Awaken to a New World

My journey from surrender to sovereignty

Helen Fisher

It is important to take care of yourself and seek any necessary guidance you feel you need when embarking on the practice of meditation.

www.helenlfisher.com

Cover design: Tina Woodcock

ISBN: 978-1-9196113-1-0

Contents

Awaken to a New World

My journey from surrender to sovereignty

My greatest hurdle was myself.
My deepest desire was to return
home to love and embody love for all.
My greatest passion is to serve
humanity.
YOU!

Introduction

Why this book? And why now?

I'm Helen Fisher, and I offer you a warm welcome into my world of observation and experience from a multidimensional perspective.

I describe myself as an energy being having a pretty bloody interesting human experience, that has, frankly, been rather colourful and continues to be. I do like a spectrum of experiences and hold a profound passion for exploring consciousness and existence. This may not be what you are used to when you first meet someone, but hey, that's me. The roles I proudly embody are mother, wife, energy intuitive, spiritual teacher, HeartMath coach and a writer. I work with mothers just like you.

My family and I began our new life in the beautiful county of Cornwall in the UK in 2018. As I share about intuition in this book, I feel it important to share with you the journey to get to my spiritual home here. This journey was totally, 100% intuitively guided and completely aligned from a much higher guidance system. This highlighted to me how I was harnessing universal manifesting skills. I will share more with you on this topic of manifesting throughout the book.

I trust that you have picked this book up through intrigue and wonder, perhaps even thinking 'what the heck is my life really about?'

I would like to suggest here that this book is the sort of book you can revisit and dip into. Each time you feel drawn to read it, it can start another healing and awakening experience within you and perhaps open you to new levels of realisations. This has been my experience.

I have written this book for the amazing mothers of energetically connected and sensitive children of the emerging new world. That is pretty much every child right now. But not only the children. Perhaps you are now a mother that was once that energetically sensitive child and have realised that you are an energetically sensitive adult, otherwise known as an empath. I invite you to sit with that for a moment. Does it resonate with you?

It rings true with me. I am one of those mothers and I was one of those children. So you could say I have written this book for the collective consciousness of mothers, and as I wrote it, I continued to have more insight and awakenings. I am delighted to share these with you here. The core of this sharing is driven by the collective consciousness of the children, and many of that collective are being labelled, in today's world, as on the spectrum.

The time is NOW to step into a new world that our children can BE. A world vibrating at the energetic level of LOVE.

As you read this book, take from it what resonates with you or lights you up and feel free to leave the rest. All I ask is that you have a willingness to read with an open mind.

There may be one question you have asked consciously, or even unconsciously, that has filtered out to merge with the universe and the answer may arrive here in this book. That could be the sole reason you have picked it up.

Warning: *I use the word 'god' in this book from time to time, along with other definitions that represent the different meanings of universal energy.*

The reason for this book is to share with you my experience of awakening to higher states of consciousness and, finally, allowing myself to fully surrender to the natural flow that serves to guide me. My journey is one of how only a spiritual way of living relieved me of my incessant, lifelong episodes of mental illness, which was monopolised by addiction and drugs as ways of numbing my very essence.

This book has my energy walking alongside you on your own journey into fully embodying a more advanced level of consciousness. It is this energy that the children already embody, and it is the epitome of freedom.

When I mention freedom, I refer to the word 'sovereignty'. Sovereignty means complete independence and self-government. As we journey through awakening our consciousness, we integrate everything about us to enable us to become a whole being, an independent being, totally responsible for ourselves and self-governing. Ultimately, to allow us to be less reliant on current systems and institutions that no longer serve us. When you become sovereign, something totally guides you from within and can access a higher intelligence. This results in the outside world serving your purpose individually and collectively.

The journey to experience sovereignty begins with surrender.

I began writing this book just before the Covid-19 pandemic struck. I knew deep in my core that this was the perfect time to write it, however the book was going to unfold.

I had a mantra as I wrote this book: 'I totally release the need to know where this writing is going and I release the need to understand the purpose of this work.' I trusted it would be revealed to me as I wrote.

As I released the need to know, I allowed a space to open up within me to have truth revealed to me. This is what I share with you on your journey. I gift to you my energetic presence and support as you move forward within these pages.

You will also notice I use the word 'quantum' throughout the book. This word refers to the energetic vibration of love, creation and a connection to the whole.

So, I'd like to ask you a question now: when you think of creation, is it something that is caged, bounded, controlled, restricted, governed and limited? Or is creation for you about freedom? Please allow yourself space and time to think about it for a moment.

As we move through these pages, you may notice how you are creation and how, unknowingly, you have kept that creation that is YOU, caged, bound, restricted and controlled.

I threaded my personal journey through this book. The journey has been one of a deep longing, a desire to always go home, to whatever and wherever that was. When I started out, I did not really understand what that meant. On many occasions, the desire to want to go home took me to the depths of wanting to check out of this life. Frequently, I found myself totally trapped within my destructive way of thinking. Eventually, through my experiences with surrender and allowing myself to delve deep within myself, I could connect with true love and creation. This experience allowed me to come to the realisation that going home was actually my journey back to love and experiencing that all-encompassing vibrational energy that we all are. This has been my transformational journey. And it can be yours too.

I set the intention and the task of writing this book purely to see written the insight that has blessed me through my life. I had not always fully acknowledged the simplicity of it until now. My intention is that by sharing my journey of awakening with you and showing you how my self-doubt and separation imprisoned me, then I can help you see your own self-imposed prison. And how you can free yourself from it.

As I jumped off the merry-go-round of suffering with my own mental health, I felt it was time to come out of the mental illness closet. It was time to take off the mask I wore that had covered up my vulnerabilities and sensitivities. By leaving the mask behind and using tools and techniques I could begin to live a life I was truly designed to live. Perhaps I can facilitate an experience for you too, to help you be free of your own inner battles causing you stress, anxiety and disconnection. And help you to really see who and what you are – YOUR TRUTH.

As I now surrender myself to the simplicity of creation and embody love, I can fully step into a new world that I know we can all fully live in.

Welcome to the new paradigm of existence.

The experience I went through and continue to go through was and is transformational, profound and completely life changing. The inner shift I experienced allows me to tap into the life that brings me the most joy, and it eradicates the belief that life is hard and a struggle.

My wish is to leave this book as a reference, a legacy for my daughter. The intention is to give her an insight into what the old world or old paradigm was like. She is a child of the new paradigm embodying love and joy. I hope that in time humanity will be present in the alternative world that is emerging now, even as I wrote this book, in the middle of the global pandemic. Or should I say the global awakening of consciousness?

To access the new world it only requires us to bring forth what is within our hearts.

I am no more special than the next person, but what I know is that I have and continue to experience the most epic of journeys with existence. I have witnessed and put into practice my innate abilities to transmute and alchemise so much energy to allow me to experience what we know as utopia. This was my journey back to LOVE. I guess I want to see that journey down on paper. If others choose to read it and it resonates or provides a space and an opportunity for a major shift to take place within you, then I know I have been of service. And I am blessed in that process.

I felt so much emotion coming through me as I wrote this book. As I surrendered and allowed the emotion to emerge, it clearly revealed to me that this book was going to take me, and potentially you, on one amazing, blessed and healing journey. This can only impact the world for the greater good, which is my number one intention. If everything is in words, you and I may experience a moment of clarity and a deeper revelation that has come from the wisdom that is held in all of us.

Whatever comes after this book is totally unknown and I let go of the outcome. The only intention I hold is that this book has its own consciousness at a high vibrational level.

You are the witness, the observer.

As we begin this journey together, I invite you to ask yourself three questions:

What does sovereignty mean to you?

What does living as a sovereign being mean to you?

And do you recognise now how you have lived in servitude or in the state of being a slave or completely subject to someone more powerful?

Truth equals freedom.

As you read this book, I invite you to allow yourself to have an experience of greater awareness and notice where you receive identification from within these words. Please feel free to just leave alone anything that does not resonate with you.

I suggest you have a journal and a pen handy as you read this book, as there will be an opportunity after each chapter to journal on a few questions I have given. They may draw you to one particular idea, or you may choose to journal on them all. There is no right or wrong here, there is only what you resonate with and choose to answer. You may also notice that your answers will change each time you revisit the questions with your journal, this serves to show you your progress of expansion.

So here I am – keeping it very simple, which didn't come naturally to me, and I will explain why later. I have tapped into the quantum field while allowing myself to write, regardless of the outcome or what you may or may not be thinking of me. There I go again: I always had a habit of doing other people's thinking for them!

Something drew you to this book, and so I hope you get at least one thing that resonates and empowers you from it.

And so we begin our journey together...

Chapter 1

Foundational Years

Old and new

M y foundational years were somewhat unstable, like most people's I guess. It wasn't until I had my daughter that I came to realise or understand how important the first seven years of life are for emotional development. I was completely oblivious to this fact. This probably explains why I had never learned the ability to self-regulate my emotions, because of the dysfunction in my early emotional development.

Please do not think that by highlighting this fact I am perpetuating the experience of being a victim and continuing to blame. I am not. That is what I have freed myself from. I am sharing the healing journey that I have allowed myself to go on, in order to be free of my struggles with mental health. I took on that role as my responsibility. By freeing myself, I free all those involved energetically to heal their own journey.

From being young, I recall that what I saw in my outside world did not quite make sense to me when I compared it to what I felt deep inside my heart. I very quickly asked questions about my existence and those questions came thick and fast. I would keep those questions mostly internalised, especially when the looks I got didn't feel supportive. The internal mind chatter resulted in them becoming what I refer to as my dementors. I developed the belief that no one had the answers. Actually, the answer was there all the time within me. Because the answers were so simple, I overlooked them as I stepped further into the complexity of my mind, developing unhelpful thinking patterns.

My childhood comprised having an acute awareness of presence and feeling a part of something much bigger than me. I would question why I was aware of everything and constantly observe people all around me, while having the question, 'why was I me and why wasn't I them?' It was a conundrum that plagued me for much of my childhood and then into adulthood. I finally realised, later in life and through heightened experiences of consciousness, that there is no separation between us. What I was experiencing was the illusion of separation from everything and everyone.

I couldn't comprehend the feeling of separation because something must have still tuned me in to the Oneness of us all. When I say 'tuned in', I mean experiencing the energy beyond the physical self, the spirit.

SEPARATION

I think that the illusion of separation really begins around the age of eight. It begs the question: did being separated from my mother early on perhaps lead me to question things much earlier? I don't know. But one thing I feel for sure is that during those foundational years we are so energetically connected to our mothers that separation can cause the feelings of disconnection and abandonment. You therefore develop beliefs that you are on your own and you have to fend for yourself if you find yourself in this situation.

The separation I experienced from my mother left an immense hole within me. It also began the process of me splitting off aspects of myself, developing personalities in order to feel accepted, and enabling the people pleaser in me. I want to really emphasise again here that this is not about sitting in blame, which is held in a victim consciousness; this is purely to give an opportunity for you to look at your own experiences with separation.

My parents separated when I was roughly the age of four or five, and although now I understand the need for that to have happened, as a small girl it turned my world upside down and inside out. The foundation I knew and relied upon had been pulled from under me and I did not have the tools, strategies or capability to deal with that process. I am very much aware that everyone involved was probably trying to do the best they could in the situation, but as a child and especially an energetically sensitive child, this was not clear to me.

Our parents are imprinted with their own patterns and programmes of behaviour unconsciously and basically repeat those patterns. As I went through healing my own feelings of abandonment, I was aware of my mother's imbedded feelings of abandonment and how her beliefs had formed from her own separation experiences early in her life. As I did my work on healing the feelings of separation, I was aware that I was also working on my mother energetically. This allows me to feel blessed knowing that the healing work I am doing is impacting my mother for the greater good on her soul journey, even if she is unaware of it, and it also empowers me to pave a freer path for the next generation – my daughter.

We are all born with a connection to source energy, but we immediately forget this and our reliance is then upon the connection energetically with our mothers. Although I was fleetingly aware of presence, it never occurred to me to ask for nurture and support in those early years. When the support and connection isn't there, then this is shown through behaviour. It was only a matter of time before I fully disconnected from everything and ran the show myself from a separated sense of self.

And so my obsession and quest in this life has been to answer the question of 'Why am I here and experiencing the presence of who I am?' What I have come to realise is that there is no 'my' – there is just presence and Oneness. Yes, that is exactly the answer and that has been shown to be true to me, having had experiences with true Oneness and expanded versions of consciousness.

The questions about existence have always been there. These became obsessional at times because of my addictive mind. I was always waiting for an answer to show up, which on reflection it did, time and time again. But I was so blinded and stuck in the ways of how I believed the answers should be shown to me. This is an example of how my thinking would try to control how everything should be through learned conditioned thinking.

My obsession with trying to find understanding for my existence took me to some very destructive places within myself. As I said to you earlier, the answers have always been there and were often very simple. I pushed the answers away because they didn't match up with what I was seeing or hearing from the people or situations outside of me. My response to these was to then develop disempowering beliefs.

Thinking about it now, I learned to doubt myself because of other people's lack of understanding in me. I created more and more experiences to validate that belief. I lost trust with my inner knowing and relied upon the outside world, which, let's face it, is pretty distorted at times.

After losing the foundation and centre of my being, I developed a strong foundation with my grandmother because I went to live with her when my parents separated. In my childhood awareness she appeared to accept me for being me, with all the weird questions I would ask her about life and death. I have memories of the times we used to walk through churchyards because I was fascinated with souls. As we enjoyed our walks together, my grandmother and I made a pact that she would contact me in some way after she left this life. We continued to talk of this throughout my adult life too. Shortly after she passed, when she transitioned from her physical body, she made contact through a medium. I continue to feel her presence now from time to time, over ten years on. Presence was something I always felt from her when we were together. I share this because on some level of consciousness, I felt we connected and perhaps understood each other from a more energetic perspective. For all I know she may well have struggled to understand me, but she certainly never showed that to me. All I ever experienced was her presence.

Perhaps you can look back on your early years and remember similar experiences with someone close to you. It doesn't have to be your parents and there are no rules in place to say who it should be, as we can have many role models and mentors in our life experience.

WHEN YOU ARE READY TO ACCEPT TRUTH, THE ANSWERS WILL BE REVEALED.

I am a simple soul that had developed a habit of complicating things. This habit allowed me to believe that if only I could master something complicated then I could validate myself as being worthy enough and clever enough for people to respect, love, see, accept and hear me. Sadly, my foundational years lacked some of those things and that was the beginning of building my own prison and only seeing what I lacked and what was wrong. There I locked myself in to the self-imposed barricades around my heart and the soul expression. Here is where I began playing out beliefs about not being good enough or being accepted or wanted. I therefore disconnected from my true essence. As part of my awakenings, I realised I was the only one that needed to see me, hear me, respect me and acknowledge me. It was not a requirement of anyone else. How could I expect those things from anyone else when I couldn't do it for myself? I did not know or understand that it was ok for me to have boundaries. Boundary teaching was not in abundance when I was younger, as it wasn't for my caregivers either. It's almost impossible to teach boundaries if you don't have them for yourself.

After having some realisations when my daughter was born in 2012 about the foundational years and also my previous awareness of knowing I was here to be a pattern changer, I could be present for her to witness who she is. I recognised my true essence mirrored back to me. I could redefine and reframe my foundational years in those moments I had with my daughter, especially when I was feeling a trigger within me. A trigger is an emotional response that can show you an unhealed trauma or condition you still hold within you. These were opportunities for me to acknowledge and begin the rebirthing process again and to integrate those aspects of my true essence I had abandoned as a child.

Many of the children being born in and around 2012 hold a consciousness of pure love and joy and as they hold that resonance they trigger within us, what no longer serves us and it is only then that we can begin building new foundations.

As I talk about the barricades and strategies I put in place to protect me, I invite you to see your own blocks and allow yourself to unlock or remove them with love. By unlocking yours, you free everyone else in the process.

I talk a lot about energy in this book, so I would like to just touch on the seven primary energy centres. These correlate to the first seven years of your life, the foundational years. You may have heard or be more familiar with the term 'chakras'. You may be completely new to this term, which is equally great, because this is a sign you are ready for new information, experiences and knowledge. You may be thinking this is all just a little bit too, oh what is the new term now, 'a bit woo woo'? This phrase makes me chuckle when I hear it because to me it isn't. When you really look into a lot of the new science and quantum physics, it really isn't 'woo woo'. Our ancestors and previous civilisations lived by the laws of nature and energy, and we are in the process of remembering this now. Personally, I love that the new science is now talking energy and in relation to us as energetic beings because it has validated so many of my life experiences. It is not just some weird stuff that no one believes. Thank god science caught up! I always felt that a time would come when we would have the balance between spirituality and science. I have a passion for both.

Anyway, I digress. So back to the foundational years. The experiences we have in the first seven years of life shape the rest of our lives. Energy as imprinting and trauma can become locked into those energy centres as blockages and patterns of potentially destructive behaviour. But do not worry – there is good news, these centres can be unlocked, allowing the release and reframing of trauma and imprints by doing energy work.

My journey to unlock and heal those blockages has led me to where I could build a completely new foundation for myself and begin living from the very beginning again. I am an adult with a new identity, which is my true soul identity and no longer the conditioned identity that is found in the ego. I will expand on this later on in the book.

I have gone through many deaths and rebirths throughout this life experience. Consciousness is forever expanding, forever being birthed, and as there is no separation, I am a fragment of the collective consciousness that is within all of us and brought into a physical manifestation. And so are YOU.

So what made me shrink? As an empathic and sensitive child I felt everything: the enormity of the fear that was present in the consciousness on the planet and the energetic fields of the people around me. I witnessed their fear and anxieties, which then gave me the feeling of wanting to shrink, constrict and preserve myself by building strategies that kept me safe. These are the very things I have had to look at and undo in order to free myself, while also honouring that, during that time, they were totally necessary. And that's ok.

As a child I had an awareness that I was not just my physical body and that the physical body was just a vessel, like a car to get me around. I was not my parents' possession, and they were simply there to guide me. I remember expressing this aloud to my mother with an unshakeable knowing. I was so sure about it. Can you recall having experiences that you just know to be true with absolutely no doubt? I realise how what I would say was perceived as quite odd, especially as the person receiving that information may not be open to those realisations as truth. It prompts me to say that it's so important to be present with the wisdom that our children bring to us through their beautiful little vessels.

No one acknowledged or understood what I expressed at that time in my life, and so I shelved that knowing within my being. That knowing never left me. It remained a hidden and a resounding truth throughout my life. A lot of my drive to find answers, new understandings, and share the truth about the children of today, comes from these experiences. I was one of those children that felt different, unsupported and misunderstood. I was seen as and told I was, a problem child, which really impacted me. The words used to label me were internalised and determined the course of my life.

As I grew up, I did not stop wondering why I was here or to witness all of this 'life stuff' happening outside me, in my outside world. The questions began and the feeling inside me grew – a feeling that I had something to do on this planet and that I was going to be part of something big. It felt like I had a big, important job to do, although I didn't know what it was, until now. I was here for NOW and the phenomenal changing times we are experiencing on the planet. I always felt and knew that I was part of something so much bigger than me, but couldn't quite put my finger on what it was. I certainly did not believe in god or religion from the way it was being presented to me.

I realised what my purpose was around the time that the Covid-19 pandemic arrived. As they announced the pandemic, every cell of my body vibrated with the internal knowing that I have felt since being young. But this time it was different. It was from an understanding of the global awakening of humanity and consciousness rather than just a virus. The virus was the catalyst. The feeling I had carried all those years now made sense from a consciousness perspective.

All I know to be true is that I felt different as a child and as an adult, resulting in feelings of loneliness, mental isolation and constantly trying to find where I could fit in. The truth of the matter was the only place I needed to fit into was my vessel and live my own truth.

That feeling of being a part of something much bigger than me has never left me and neither has my desire, or my want, to just go home to where I came from. Something has deeply embedded these feelings in my being. This knowing that I have a purpose and a mission in this incarnation has driven me forward through all the trials and tribulations, the suffering of depressions, anxiety, suicidal thoughts and battles with addictions. This knowing assured me that one day it would end and the truth would be revealed. And I'm delighted to tell you that through my journey back to love, I now feel I am at home.

In 2012, after birthing my daughter, my journey of unravelling began.

It was so timely as I was aware of the shift in consciousness taking place on the planet from this time. You may have heard about the prophecies of the end of the world in 2012, but I invite you to look at this from the Mayan calendar perspective if you are new to this.

As I watched the consciousness of my baby unfold, I saw 'me' from an evolutionary perspective. Not for one minute did I believe I could be a person who embodied LOVE and have compassion for myself and nurture myself, instead of self-destructing daily. My self-destructive thought patterns and behaviours, which were my normal at the time, were all I knew. I identified with my conditioned internal narrative from childhood. And yet, here I was, feeling for the first time the energy of love in my heart, and I faced the realisation that I could now begin to change those patterns. As I began to parent my baby girl, I parented myself too.

It's now time for you to allow yourself to step fully into love and be. And perhaps now it is time to allow your child or children to be fully who they are without imposing too many outdated structures and conditions on to them. This process is a work in progress, I might add.

As I went through my breakdown of the old self and foundation, I birthed the new identity of who I was, fully embodying my soul essence. I started life again, building a new identity based on my truth. And let me tell you – it's very exciting. It has reignited the wonderment within me, like a child discovering everything for the first time and being able to create new things from the energy of love and joy. I know I can play a big part by adding to the collective consciousness of many other mothers that are paving the way for a brighter future for the children that is nothing like we have seen before. The old has to go. We have to bring forth the new world with a new foundation based on love, joy and compassion.

There is no end to experience, there is only constant growth, expansion and transformation based on consciousness.

As we take this journey, we see another world and the new paradigm emerge from our awakened consciousness. We are a collective and we are sovereign. We can create the world we want to see. It's time.

Stop waiting for someone to do it for you. Begin by putting the new foundations in place.

THE TIME IS NOW!

Journal

I invite you to now spend some quiet time to reflect on your own foundational years. Write down a particular age or ages that you feel had pivotal moments. Perhaps you also experienced some trauma and you can see where it has continued throughout your life in different ways.

If you could recreate your foundational years and parent yourself, how would you do it differently?

How are you parenting now? And does that reflect in what you have answered with the above questions? If it doesn't, go ahead and ask yourself why that is. What are the blocks in place for you parenting in the way you really desire?

Be as honest as you can, even if it feels uncomfortable. The more honest you can be with yourself, the freer you become.

Fears

False evidence appearing real

Fear, especially now, serves only to disconnect us from ourselves, each other and our innate ability to connect into higher levels of consciousness and source energy. For us to really connect on every level, we must have an experience of surrender.

It is so easy to be absorbed by our own desperation that we see no way out, riddled with fear and anxiety, with the constant mental chatter which does not serve us. When the mental chatter is loud, it is almost impossible to access solutions. Those solutions can be found by tapping into the heart intelligence or source energy. They are one and the same.

I was frequently in fear of taking action that I was unfamiliar with, especially when faced with the unknown or uncertainty because I had so many 'what ifs' and lacked the ability to believe that I could deal with anything. Frequently I got to where my life depended on letting go of the fear.

I mentioned earlier that I happened to be writing this book during an experience we all share – a pandemic. I am not here to discount the nature of the pandemic. I prefer to witness the experience from a much broader perspective, as I have been gifted with this ability. Sometimes this perspective can be a burden. I see this experience as a huge global awakening of humanity and consciousness, and it is time we all stepped into the vibration of love. These times we are in now are truly transformational, and we could create a new world in which we are all sovereign beings. We are going through an evolutionary leap and during any transformation, it can get a little ugly when the old way is breaking down and the alternative path is filtering in. As we evolve from the inside, we are going to see the breakdown of the old in the outside world.

Fear and anxiety are at their peak. As I write this, I can see those feelings have escalated in many of all ages. I work continuously on changing fears into something else because I would not be human if I didn't experience them, however spiritual and full of love I am. It's easy for the ego to be in a state of denial and convince you that you are not in fear about 'stuff' because you have to appear to be all clued up on this spiritual path. I'm going to tell you here and now – sorry, but that is BS from my experience. When one is enduring internal chaos, anxiety and fear, it is very difficult to see that there is a solution. But there is absolutely an answer, and it starts with surrender, connection and collaboration. My mother once profoundly said to me in one of my great times of struggle, 'There is always a solution.' And that has always stuck with me.

For such a long time, the outside world has inundated us with information and disinformation to the point of mental overload. We have not been given or necessarily had access to the techniques to navigate a world that has reached its maximum capacity to sustain itself energetically. It is now time to fully integrate a fresh way of creative thinking that comes from felt perceptions. This will enable us to fully be. It's time we allowed ourselves to feel again.

It's natural to have fears. After all, our systems as human beings hold the DNA that our ancestors held and because of this we lived in the state of fight or flight for a long time. Many people now are constantly in this state of fight or flight. And because it's a constant state or feeling, it's very hard to recognise when you are in it until you have some reprieve. The time we are living in now is triggering feelings of powerlessness and ramping up the lioness streak in us to protect our children. There is a level of fear for what sort of world we are leaving for our children. I am trying to raise my child to be a sovereign being who isn't limited in her creation while having her own boundaries in place in order to stay true to herself. The feelings of powerlessness are all absolutely normal to have. As a mother I am not immune from these feelings, I just know that we can turn powerlessness into power by connecting in with a higher source for true guidance and access higher levels of consciousness. These levels of awareness can help us create a future we want to see for our children, one that comes from a much higher serving and loving place.

So how do we alchemise that fear into something else? Alchemy means to transform the nature of something by a seemingly magical process. Allow yourself for a moment to acknowledge that you are a magical being. We alchemise through the presence of love, which means accessing the heart's intelligence.

When we hold the energy of fear, we see and experience that fear mirrored back to us from the outside world. We project outwards our level of consciousness to the world. Therefore, the work we do to change our level of consciousness is done on the inside of us. There the energy changes and what we experience on the outside world will mirror our inner reality, resulting in seeing a different world, our world. The transformations take place from the inside.

Stop waiting for the outside world to change, it begins with you.

Surrendering to the fear is where a shift in energy within you can take place. The experience of surrendering can happen in a moment; it's not something you have to schedule into your busy routine to actively do. Surrendering is not about doing – it's a state of being. The reason I am so passionate about surrender and want to share my experience with other mothers is to help relinquish the inner power struggle that is generated by so much fear and anxiety held within. These can be your own personal fears or a collective fear that you are perhaps picking up on energetically, especially if you are an empath or sensitive person. We pick up these feelings throughout our chakras, which then impacts our nervous system, endocrine system and immune system. They infiltrate every aspect of our being, blocking us from being connected to our very core, our higher self, the universe, god source.

The experience of fear is exacerbated by what we feed our consciousness on a daily basis, and the result can be feelings of powerlessness and hopelessness.

The media can play a huge part in creating experiences of fear and anxiety.

When I was in my early twenties, I came to realise that what I was witnessing in the mainstream media portrayed a world monopolised by fear, anger and hatred. This led me to ask the question: why were we only being shown those aspects? What I was watching fed and triggered the imprinted beliefs, the ones I held about not feeling safe, which then kept me in a psychological loop of constantly feeling unsafe. What we believe, we will see. And we are certainly seeing the fear campaign ramping up now during the pandemic.

At some point in 2020, I had a moment when a question popped into my awareness. The question was, 'What would really happen if I totally stepped away from following any of the mainstream media?' Followed by another: 'What would really happen to me?' (I will give you an opportunity to journal on this question at the end of this chapter.) While I haven't been one to sit and watch the news or mainstream television for a few years now, I dipped in and out of it for updates on the pandemic. Doing this, I came to realise that what I was witnessing was just one narrative that was filling me with fear. And this reminded me of previous fears that had taken me into a state of feeling powerless and were controlling me.

I then realised that the recent programming from this one narrative was contributing to controlling the masses into believing something that was not 100% true on many levels. It was only serving to keep most people in a state of fear. Just to remind you, when we are in a state of fear, we are disconnected and our behaviours towards each other represents that internal condition. We turn that fear onto one another, very subtly, which then chips away at our mental health, not only in adults but in our children too.

Furthermore, we are inundated with subliminal programming everywhere. What we hear or see, even the symbols that are used, activate a vibration in our energy field. When this triggers the fear response within our brain, we end up being in what is called 'fight or flight' mode. We witness the world from that state of being. For example, when I am having fearful thoughts and feelings, I believe I am not safe in the world and everyone is out to cause me harm. This means I am giving all of my power away, which comes more often than not from some experiences in childhood. Now, when I use various techniques and change my negative beliefs into ones that are aligned with love, compassion, gratitude and understanding, I can see the outside world from that state of being as I feel balanced and more empowered to respond from that state.

What I am saying to you here is that you always have the power within you to shift the experience you want to have in this world, despite what you may or may not be told to do. Rather than listening to what you are constantly being told to do, you could ask yourself the question, 'How would I like to be in this moment?' By doing so, you have the power to choose your state of being and what you contribute to the outside world from a more aligned and coherent space within you. You have the ability and the right to question everything. You probably hold some mental programming within you that tells you not to question anything and just accept what you are being told, with the belief that it is in your best interest. By questioning this belief, you can rediscover your ability to discern what truth is for you, and especially your child. Discernment can be experienced when you surrender the fear. It is a powerful tool to embody.

So let's take the next step forward and surrender.

Note: *The word 'surrender' will crop up throughout this book. It is a constant act, not just one episode. To expand and grow to higher versions of yourself, you must surrender and let go many times.*

Journal

Allow yourself to breathe into the heart space for a few moments. Shift your attention and focus on your heart or chest area and breathe in and out evenly and consistently. As you become present in the heart, ASK the following questions one at a time to your heart intelligence:

1. What world would I like to SEE?

2. How would I like to FEEL on a daily basis?

3. How would I like to BE in this moment?

4. What would really happen if I totally stepped away from following any of the mainstream media? What would really happen to me?

Write what comes to mind without overthinking it.

CHAPTER 3

Reality

The quality or state of being real

What is your reality right now? This is probably an appropriate time to ask you this question, given what the outside world looks like and how you may feel and be affected by it.

The reality I often used to experience showed me one thing, and that was the act of surrender, in order to really step into and feel my innate ability to consciously choose a reality I actually wanted. Before having these surrender experiences and mini awakenings, my realities were mostly manifesting from an unconscious state of being.

The beauty to be found in the process of surrender is fundamentally divine. This has been my experience and I would love it to be yours too.

I looked up some definitions of 'surrender' in the dictionary, and there are various meanings. The definition I most identify with and have experienced is:

'Abandoning oneself entirely to a powerful emotion or influence.'

(Webster's Dictionary)

This powerful influence was the divine presence that immediately flowed through me following the act of surrender.

Your thoughts are where the journey begins. Identify whether the thoughts you are having are actually your organic thoughts that are serving your creation or whether they are coming from a mental programming that you are running in your subconscious. Once you can surrender your thoughts, you can create a different reality by telling a different story.

The reason my surrender experiences happened was because I was ready for them after feeling broken and realising alone that I did not have the answers or solutions to my life. It was then that the all-pervading force that is within me and encrypted within us all had one purpose: to show itself and enable me to experience the fullest magnitude of who we all are. The force that is LOVE.

The act of surrender is similar each time, but the result of each surrender reveals something different and, at times, more profound insights.

Life happens for you and not to you from the vantage point of surrender.

Stop what you are doing now and ask yourself; What is my reality NOW?' Observe how quickly your mind grasps at any potential conditioning to answer that question. By default, the answer will want to come from the conditioned, ego-based world it has led you to believe in, the story you have constantly been telling yourself and subsequently reacting to.

My journey with surrender highlights how time and time again I was presented with an opportunity or a portal into my very core. A bit like the idea of a journey to the centre of the earth. As there is no separation between our being and the very core of the earth, it is quite an accurate description. The journey of surrender not only allows me to connect with everything but also gives me the opportunity to see every possible aspect of my quantum self. From here I can jettison my being to a completely different dimension and bring forth a newer version of consciousness.

Of course, at any moment I also have the choice to go back into a lower ego dimension or perspective, at any point I wish to. That is the power of choice and free will. However, the lower dimensions I find rather unpleasant now.

I used to have a continuous experience of battling with the very life force that was only there to guide me. My focus, because of early mind programming, was always on the outside world and being in a constant state of reaction to it. Because I had disconnected from my inner self, I trusted only what was on the outside of me and had forgotten that I could trust my inner guidance system, my gut instincts. So I was constantly creating a reality by reacting unconsciously to whatever was going on around me. As a young girl, I believed everything from the people that were put on my path to guide me. I learned to ignore my instincts by suppressing them. Yes, there are those that guide us and guide us well, but there are those that try to guide us through power, control and wrong (and often disconnected) information. Everyone is there to teach us in some way as a reflection and present an opportunity to go within and ask ourselves the right questions.

I'd like to share with you my first experience with surrender and highlight that there is some discussion of drug use, because addiction has played a huge role in my life and my surrenders.

SURRENDERING TO CREATE REALITY

My very first experience of surrender was at the age of 26. At this point there was certainly no conscious choice or willingness to surrender, only a necessity if I were to continue my life beyond this point. This surrender was also not intentional or driven by a knowing of what the outcome would be if I surrendered. No – this was a universally enforced surrender because of a higher part of me willing to live. In one way the willingness was there, but just not in the way I thought. I was almost spiritually dead and in the deepest and darkest depression I had ever experienced at that point. Let's face it, I didn't even know what surrender meant in relation to this experience, let alone to use it regularly in my vocabulary or practice it as a way of being and living.

On this occasion, the life experience that brought me to my knees, or point of surrender if you prefer, was me using a cocktail of drugs. I did this to help me function on a day-to-day basis and quieten the constant mental noise that was, on reflection, designed to destroy me. I just wanted the internal narrative and emotional pain I felt, wrapped up in a whole load of resentments that I held, to end and stop. My solution then was to use drink and drugs. They appeared to be my only salvation, and the mixture worked. Using recreational drugs is how the false illusion of freedom started. It was the way I would make the internal noise stop and it provided the potential for me to experience complete oblivion by exiting a reality I did not want to be in.

When I started to take drugs, it was purely for the enjoyment factor, until I liked it too much. I realised that the more I took, the less I had to focus on reality, the pressures of life and living with the constant internal battles I was having. My reality was perfect on drugs, or so I thought, until I understood that I couldn't stop even if I wanted to. Here was the beginning of a reaction I was having to the substances. It wasn't until later in my life that I learned of the sensitivity I had, the disease of addiction that I suffered with, and the inability to stop because of this. I was blind to the amount of emotional baggage I was carrying around with me and I wasn't even aware of what it comprised. Neither was I aware of the amount of internal anger I had, which I only turned into myself, and was damaging me. I couldn't deal with it because I wasn't equipped with the ability to self-regulate my emotions without self-medicating. As I mentioned before, your caregivers cannot show you something they lacked, as they weren't shown or supported in their own upbringing. I now only hold compassion for this fact and my caregivers.

There were a lot of dark times and some profoundly enlightening experiences with my drug taking. I'll be honest, I loved taking certain drugs that opened up expansive levels of consciousness for me. The other drugs just sent me on a downward spiral to hell, especially the ones that I had become severely addicted to and just could not stop consuming.

It seems a crazy way to think, to even go there, talking about a 'good' side to an experience of drugs, but I will elaborate my reasoning for this. There are currently many people who choose plant medicines to enter the same experiences I had. At the time, I did not know that choosing to experiment with drugs would cause the amount of information I would receive into my consciousness from a multidimensional level. But it certainly answered a lot of my internal lifelong questions and validated the innate belief I held from childhood of not just being a physical body.

It is important to point out what the experiences I had while taking certain drugs showed me. It's really only now that I can integrate those experiences into my true being as a natural way of living, without having to use drugs. I am a multidimensional being, as we all are, with vast levels of consciousness available to me. And it's time we all remembered and experienced that.

What I was seeking while taking drugs was a connection with something – I realise that more than ever now. Time to connect, to be in my own free-flowing mind and to have the freedom to express myself without a care in the world. And most importantly, to not care what people might think of me. Ultimately, I connected to my essence, to me.

Connection is what we all collectively strive for in life and is one of the fundamental basics of existence. To really stand in our own truth without a care about what anyone else may think or judge us for. Seeking total freedom.

While taking drugs, I would relish the opportunity to lose all inhibitions and be who I really was. I could fully connect with another person as if they were me because they were actually an aspect of me, a mirror of me in that 'now' moment if you will.

But – and here's the but – I would wake up the next day after taking drugs with a sudden panic and bang! There was reality, consciousness!

Yes, there was a reality that I didn't like at the time because I struggled to be the me that I was when I was free to express myself while on the drugs. Free from the mind chatter and destructive thought patterns and programmes. Here is an example of creating my reality from my thoughts.

When the drugs had run out, the fear started to creep in and the reality I was used to every day came back. Was I choosing that reality or was it coming from the unconscious? This is important. I want to highlight to you how our subconscious and the unconscious programming create your reality. We are creative beings, so we are creating all the time.

It's odd to think now that to get back to being completely at one with myself, my pure, expressive and loving soul, I had to almost kill myself. Or kill the very vessel that allowed me to experience the wonderful aspect of life that I was. The more I used drugs, the more I was prolonging my unbearable reality, and this was usually the reality that I didn't want to live. And so I took the drugs to escape.

When the drugs ran out, they would leave me living in fear more and more. I could not cope and my body reacted by shutting down. I would go into survival mode physically, mentally and spiritually, otherwise known as 'fight or flight'. Notice I don't mention 'emotionally' here as I didn't even know what it was to feel. I was inundated with warning signs to change my behaviour, but I was unable to see a way out. It became a slippery slope to disaster and all because I wanted that moment of freedom, to be who I truly am without judgement.

The only way to experience that freedom was through chemical influences. Sadly, this is a familiar story for many people, probably now in our times more than in any other in history with the ready availability of pharmaceutical and recreational drugs. I thank something much bigger than me for the fact that I am still here and have been able to write these words. Many aren't so lucky, and many more are struggling right now.

Around 20 years ago I realised that certain drugs I was using were, somehow, activating an opening of some sort within me and the only way I can describe it is that it was allowing me to become closer to the universe/source/god. At the time it felt like something above my head was opening which allowed me to see the bigger picture, expanded consciousness, the universe and that everything was all right. Everything is wonderful and everybody is love. The experience was amazing. I loved that I could witness the greatness in everyone and the fear, hate, jealousy, etc. just disappeared. Not only did I have the ability to see, but I became aware of everyone else who was also experiencing this as a collective energy. That's when I wanted to find out how I was experiencing this and how we could all live this way for ever.

I wasn't aware of the energy centres called chakras at that time, but I was suddenly guided and directed to begin to understand them. Now I find it fascinating how I labelled the crown chakra as a trapdoor because at that dark time in my life I most certainly felt trapped daily. As this chakra opened, I felt the freedom that I so desired in every moment of this life.

The crown chakra is right on the top of the head, and when this chakra is open and spinning, the energy can flow in. We are all energy, balls of energy connected to the universe, connected to everything. I became trapped within my physical self or mental conditioning and experienced endless insecurities, fear and hatred. These are all ego-based identities, full of conditions and programming. I was totally unaware of this at that point, until I began an awakening process.

My ingrained belief was programmed to see that life was hard and a struggle, because that was how it was for our elders. When you repeatedly hear life is hard, it sticks and you do not question it, you just accept it. Another inbuilt belief was not to question anything, just do as you are told. This is scary when you think about it, and certainly if you put it into the context of recent times. Actually, we must question everything.

We're taught to look up to our peers, those in authority and those that are there to guide us when we are young, aren't we? We don't tend to think that what they are telling us is coming from their own inbuilt programming. Unless they have had some profound awakening, they are just going to pass down their programming.

This is not always intentional; it is often unconsciously passed on.

When I was on certain drugs, all the constraints and inbuilt boundaries disappeared and I could experience being who I truly was. That was a beautiful, pure energy form that only knows LOVE. I relished the experience of having no fear of my own self-expression. Then when the trapdoor opened, I would soar into another stratosphere. I found myself able to connect like never before and be one with every other energetic being and the universal phenomena. My burning question was always: can chemicals really just be the cause of this or is there something much bigger going on here?

Although I had studied anatomy and physiology in the past, I can truly say I really didn't fully understand the body's biological systems or my body because I was totally disconnected from it for most of my life. I certainly learned nothing about the energy of the body, which now makes so much sense to me through my integration work and my own experiences of integrating into my body. Chemicals, in some ways, allow you to open this flow of consciousness, and I experienced that. Now I know this consciousness to be the quantum field. It wasn't until the trapdoor opened that I understood the system and how my energy and consciousness are connected to it. I understood how I could use this vessel for greater awareness, connection to higher consciousness and self-regulating. Therefore, I can consciously create a reality and a world I want to exist in. We can all initiate chemical reactions within our bodies to expand our consciousness using the heart.

The positive experiences of experimenting with drugs at the time showed me the release and the freedom I could have.

As I reflect now, what I was actually experiencing was Oneness for the first time, but through the use of chemicals. It wasn't until I was in my forties that I would experience pure Oneness, without any chemicals influencing that experience, all natural. I will share more with you about Oneness later, but for now let's talk a bit more about the chakras.

THIRD DIMENSIONAL CHAKRAS

I would like to offer you a brief description of the seven primary chakras, or energy centres. I highly recommend you begin your own journey of learning, understanding and applying the use of your own chakras. See for yourself the transformations you can have. Experience is true knowledge.

I will not stay too long on these because later on I will invite you to go into the higher dimensional chakras, which we are now beginning to activate and use as we embark on our evolutionary leap in human consciousness and embodying them. Just for now, as you progress through the book, allow yourself to begin a little practice with each of these chakras in meditation.

We know the seven primary chakras as the third dimensional chakras. They all have a colour frequency.

ROOT CHAKRA
COLOUR: red
POSITION: base of the spine
This is the chakra of stability, security and our basic needs. When this chakra is open, we feel safe and fearless.

SACRAL CHAKRA
COLOUR: orange
POSITION: sacrum
This chakra is responsible for creative expression and is our sexual centre.

SOLAR PLEXUS CHAKRA
COLOUR: yellow
POSITION: solar plexus
This chakra is the source of your personal power.

HEART CHAKRA
COLOUR: green
POSITION: middle of the chest
This is the connection between the lower chakras of matter and the upper chakras of spirit. The heart chakra is our source of love and connection.

THROAT CHAKRA
COLOUR: blue
POSITION: throat
This chakra is the source of our verbal expression and the ability to speak our highest truth.

THIRD EYE CHAKRA
COLOUR: indigo
POSITION: middle of the forehead
This chakra is the centre of our intuition.

CROWN CHAKRA
COLOUR: purple
POSITION: top of the head
This is the chakra of enlightenment and spiritual connection, where we can access our higher selves, others and ultimately the divine.

The act of surrender in my twenties looked to the outside world like me physically and mentally being unable to get out of bed or even have any impetus to live. I literally had nothing left inside me. The only thing I could do was swallow any pride I had left. So I picked up the phone to my mother and asked her to come and get me from where I was living in London. In that moment, my world and reality as I knew them dissolved and for the first time, I had no ability to mentally project into the future. Now, with hindsight, I know that this was a moment of freedom in itself. It completely immersed me in the unknown. I had no future; I only had the moment I was in.

It stripped me of everything I knew at that point. I had to stop working; I had to leave the close friend and the home we were living in, and I had no money. I was literally an empty vessel of a self, a blank canvas. You could say I was spiritually dead. I transported this vessel of mine back to the family home to begin my journey of recovery. I had entered a place of nothingness and an unknown, but at the time I wasn't aware of that. It's not until recently that I have understood what a truly powerful place that is to be in, to begin creation afresh.

I was in a state of recovery from my total breakdown or as I prefer to call it, a spiritual awakening, for just under a year. However, I'm sad to say that within that year I was still consuming pharmaceutical painkillers and alcohol, alongside antidepressants, sleeping tablets and beta blockers. It was a real cocktail. I did not need the painkillers for anything specific. I later realised how my illness of addiction manifested itself and it was in the form of opiates. I did not have the ability to control the situation on my own due to a sensitivity I had, so no amount of willpower was going to make me stop. What I find fascinating now is how all these chemicals I was consuming are all still seen as perfectly acceptable in society. I am not knocking the fact that there is indeed a time and a place for certain medications, but they are not the only solution, as I was to find out later in my journey.

I refer to my recovery process as a spiritual awakening. Medically, it is often referred to as a nervous breakdown. And yes, it was a total breakdown of my nervous system. It was shot to pieces, which I did not understand at the time. I can see now how so many of us are running unknowingly on overstimulated nervous systems until we find ourselves at the doctor's for medication because of increased levels of anxiety. So what I was going through was an awakening process and a total breakdown. Take a look at humanity now on a global scale and witness the breaking down as part of a larger awakening process.

Fundamentally we are energetic beings first, so when I view it from that point, why would I not believe it to be an awakening of consciousness? I had, after all, spent my entire life allowing myself to believe all sorts of rubbish, but this belief of being energetic first came from my very core.

As my self-will came back into full force and I felt better, I thought I could run my life again on my ideas. This was mostly coming from unconscious programming again. Little did I know that this programming was orchestrating my next surrender. I had therapy sessions, but clearly these did nothing to undo any programming that I was unconsciously still running in my head. You would think that after having the first experience of surrender and reaching the depths of depression I would not have picked up any recreational drugs again... that would just be insane, wouldn't it? Well, guess what? The old pattern played out again! Self-will reached its peak once again and the willingness to surrender was about to prevail, again.

Fast forward now to my early thirties and I found myself having yet another moment of surrender. This time I literally fell to my knees one night in the bathroom and asked out loud for someone to help me. I was wrapped up, bound if you like, in a feeling of desperation, loneliness, powerlessness and hopelessness. A knowing that I was potentially going to be dead soon.

And yet the profound thing here was, this time, I found myself in a state of willingness to ask for the help and energetically I had put myself into a space of being opened to receiving that help. This was driven by the energy of intention as I had nothing of me left, again. This second surrender was because of a severe addiction to painkillers prescribed by my doctor, and as I suffered with the disease of addiction, I could not stop just by using my own willpower, no matter how I tried. Many people do not understand the nature of true addiction. Therefore, there is so much judgement around those who suffer with this mental and physical illness.

As I look back on my experiences with my own GP and his role in my addiction, it saddens me that he also didn't fully understand addiction. I viewed him a bit like I would view a drug dealer on the streets. I recall occasions when my GP would ask me to help him understand addiction while he continued to offer me prescriptions, despite me saying I needed help weaning off. Had I not had the desperation and willingness to wean off, I would have been snatching those prescriptions out of his hand. It was at those points that I knew I needed help from family members too, to moderate what I was taking to be able to wean off.

I point out the concepts of willingness, asking and receiving, and we will cover them in further reflections later on in the book. But suffice to say during that time I didn't see or understand how the important universal laws were at play. I understand them to be important NOW.

And one other thought to add: the reason I talk about my drug experiences is that those are the episodes that have taught me so much about consciousness, who we are as energy beings and the power that is connected to the god source.

Even now I can often forget that I handed my will over and wonder why I end up being 'smashed to pieces' because the universe is trying to bring to me the very thing I have asked for! That is a higher will being shown to me. And frankly, the higher will really must shine now through everyone in order to experience a free world.

I had to come to a point where I was ready to allow myself to see the pathway in a more aligned way and integrate it into my very being as my new reality. So what was actually stopping me? I realise now that this was the deep, imprinted unconscious belief structures and conditioning that kept showing themselves and running my previous life. I would fall back to sleep into the unconscious.

7-DAY CHAKRA-OPENING MEDITATION

Have your journal to hand to write down any experiences you may encounter during the meditations. Not everyone is a visual person, so with these meditations it's important to highlight that intention is enough as you go through the process of opening up the chakras. All experiences you have are valid, however strange they may appear.

MEDITATION

Sit quietly with the bottom of your feet on the ground.

Begin breathing slowly and a little more deeply than usual, and keep the breath consistent as you breathe in and out. Take your time to allow your breath to get into a rhythm.

Begin to shift your attention and focus to the root chakra. I invite you to set your intention to see the colour red or anything that represents the colour red, for example, a postbox, etc. As you are with the colour red, allow yourself to see the root chakra spinning clockwise. Again, intending to see it or even sense it is enough.

Be aware of any sensations you may feel in your body.

For many people, beginning to feel or sense is a whole new experience. There is no right or wrong with this, there is only your experience.

During the following days, do the same for the remaining six chakras that you have done with the root chakra. Remember to just pick one chakra each day using the specific colour for the chakra you are choosing to work on.

GROUNDING

When you have finished the meditation each day, allow yourself to move your energy into the planet. This can be simply done by imagining the planet below you and roots coming out of your feet and going into the planet. We know this as 'grounding'. It's good to get into this habit when you are opening up your chakras.

Journal

What did you sense? This can come from feeling, seeing or/and hearing. Did you have any insights and revelations?

Doing the chakra exercises can open you up to more felt perception, and this is where you can begin to experience your truth and also maybe notice any blocked energy centres.

CHAPTER 4

Ego

Edging god out

Let's begin to talk about the ego and how we make friends with it. Perhaps we might begin the journey to transcend the ego through more surrender and explore how the ego has previously edged out god. This is where we can really explore the patterns of behaviour and the beliefs we hold and where we have learned to cast blame in order to disconnect us further from what is actually true in our essence or god consciousness. Remember that god consciousness makes up the essence of who we are.

Let me explain, in simple terms, what the ego is. It is not something to completely rid ourselves of, but it is something to understand and integrate into our very being. All of our inner battles come from the ego being separate and dominant for a long time. The ego is your thoughts, or incessant thoughts in my case, and programmes installed in your mind that you ultimately build your identity from. For many the ego can be called the monkey mind: that little monkey sitting on your shoulder, keeping you small and trying to control everything, making you believe you will be safe if you follow its thought process. My experience of continually living by my mental thoughts only leads to my own entrapment and imprisonment. Nobody could actually do that to me – but I held a belief that what I was hearing or seeing was true. Therefore, looking at your beliefs is so important and can transform your life.

Before my first experience with surrender, I felt separated and disconnected on the inside of me, like I was a complete void, and I had convinced myself via my thoughts that no one really cared that much about me, anyway. I would be better off dead. I was trapped in self-pity and in what we know as victim consciousness. It wasn't that no one really cared about me; it was that I didn't care about me because I had lost all connection to who I was. This sort of thinking has been a common characteristic leading up to all of my surrender experiences.

This belief in my lack of connection fuelled my ability to take the continuous path of self-destruction. That button was being pressed very firmly to the point of potential death. These were subconscious beliefs that had been imprinted into my very core from being young, and they became my story that was on constant repeat. It was like a computer software programme running repeatedly in my head and became my very being. When people said, 'just let it go,' it always baffled me how people did that because I did not know how to let go and got increasingly frustrated because I couldn't. Not that I didn't want to, I just couldn't and didn't know how to. I later realised that the letting go process had to come from a different level of consciousness. I couldn't think my way to letting go because obsessive, destructive thinking was my problem.

This is where I became addicted to the drugs and other methods of numbing myself. There were so many. At the time it seemed my only solution to free myself and to let go of the feelings of anger, hatred for myself, frustration, fear of what people think, etc. I was the perfect example of how I became caged in by my own fear and imperfections because someone else's life always seemed so perfect and I couldn't possibly live up to that. I fell into the trap of comparison.

Before my surrenders and in the thick of my addictions, I was constantly feeding the problem of self-destruct by the feelings and beliefs I held for myself. I hated the person I had turned into, but knew deep in the essence of my heart that this was not the true me. In my active addiction I had sneaky behaviour to get more drugs and not let anyone else know, so the unconscious self could consume it all.

Now I can see that this behaviour can be linked to the whole global experience of consumerism that we are all enslaved by. There are many addictions that are not chemical or prescription-drug-based – there is addiction to shopping, spending, eating, alcohol, people. The list is long. But because they appear to be socially acceptable, it is difficult to see the damage until you awaken to it. I had become someone who would tell lies and make up stories that I actually believed and convinced myself of in order to get hold of drugs. I knew I couldn't go on living this lie and betraying the people I cared about. I knew I was not this person. My ego was convincing me and had tapped into that deep knowing inside. In that moment I experienced an awakening and I knew something had to change. I was willing to do something different and look at how my ego was driving me so unconsciously. God consciousness is felt through the heart and as I was living so much in my ego, the lies it would tell me resulted in the lies appearing true and edging god out.

Did you know you have the ability to change your belief in any given moment? I invite you to stop reading and sit quietly for a minute or two with what I have just said. I'll say it again, you can change your belief in any given moment. And then what you believe you will begin to see. Does that feel empowering to you?

Let's also talk about my version of depression; everyone's version is unique. The only way I can describe my experience of depression is it was like falling into a complete void, emptiness, nothingness and darkness. It's like something is telling you that you need to take yourself out of that existence that you know and step back to re-evaluate your life and rebirth. For me it was a big black cloud hovering above my head together with a big black hole I could see myself slipping down, faster and faster, desperately trying to grip onto something. It was so easy to go with the negativity because I felt that's all there was, I couldn't access any hope. I had no strength whatsoever to fight, and all I wanted to do was stay under my duvet cover and sleep forever.

The constant lows of my depressions were because I would beat myself up and hated myself because I had to turn to drugs to make myself feel good or just feel different. They helped me to believe that people would like me, and I would be able to express myself, to switch off the outside world or my perception of the outside world that I had created. I thought about suicide so many times, but I didn't have the guts to do anything about it. Yet it always seemed to be the best way out. During those dark thoughts, other feelings of knowing would also surface. These thoughts and feelings that I'd had from being a child, a kind of innate knowing that I had always held, told me I could not check out now or any other time. Because I have a mission in this life and I cannot leave until it is done.

You may wonder what I mean by having a mission in life. You may also resonate with what I have said about having a mission in this life. Allow me to explain a little further about this mission. It became clearer to me on my spiritual journey that I was what is termed as a lightworker. Lightworkers are pretty much what it says on the tin. We work for the light and shine a light into the darkness. We channel the light energetically and we can do this in various forms, depending on our particular role in this incarnation.

The deep sense I felt from being very young was that I was here to experience something big on this planet, and I had a big job to do. I absolutely know that to be true now as the time came when all of that became the reality – the day the pandemic struck. There are many other lightworkers, who understand this sense of mission, of being part of the global awakening to higher states of consciousness and to live on a planet creating from that level of consciousness. My role is to assist others, especially mothers, to be in that higher state too. These are the times we are in now as I write this book and why I write this book.

There was no way I could carry on with my life the way it was. This was an opportunity for surrender to present itself. I have suffered depression so many times to different extremes, some worse than others. But now each time I experience them, I can recognise the signs and choose a practise of surrender to allow in a higher guidance to guide me through.

The fact about addiction is that in this case the drugs are just the symptom. It wasn't necessarily the drugs that took me on a path to destruction; it was actually my own thinking that took me on that path. All I had to do was reach for something that would relieve me of that painful place within myself. I needed relief, and I needed to feel something different. The drugs would then compound the experience and not only begin to destroy my physical vessel but also numb the most powerful part of me – my heart, my emotions and where the source of my connection is.

After the first experience of surrender, I got to a point that I was feeling better, although I was still in a state of victim consciousness. This state felt safe to me then, as I was firmly embedded in the breakdown's trauma experience I had just gone through. Sitting in this trauma felt like a sense of security. I clearly had more healing work to do, but I did not know that at the time. However, I needed to get my life back together, and this meant going back to work, and it was a frightening prospect because I had to leave my safe cocoon.

So here is the first example of what I mean by repeating unconscious patterns. I decided I would go back to London. I also decided that it would be totally ok to consume a tiny amount of recreational drugs because I felt better and believed it would be ok this time. But during this episode I had a very profound experience, as I had a physical adverse reaction to the drugs I had taken. It was the classic reaction that you might have heard of where the body overheats; you vomit and other unpleasant things. I was aware of being in an altered state of consciousness. During this experience I was actually out of linear time and I had what I can only describe as an energetic conversation with what appeared to be a group of entities. But not in a crazy alien way!

These entities felt to me like a council of some sort, whether that be what I knew of as the karmic council or, as I now understand as, a galactic council. They said to me that I was at a point where I had to make a choice either to go on as I am and die, there and then, or to go back and begin to follow the path I had chosen in this life to help others, which had been my passion. So just to paint the picture further for you, in the physical realm while I was having this experience, two of my friends sat either side of me, holding me up as my physical body was expelling the poison I had put into it. They were considering calling an ambulance. As I made the conscious choice to live the path I had chosen, I snapped out of the state I was in and sat bolt upright as if nothing had happened. And I was fine. This was a very weird experience for my friends. What was interesting to me during this experience, was the fact that I had spent so much of my life from childhood not wanting to be here and when I faced an opportunity to exit this life, I chose not to. Fascinating, hey?

This experience only added value to my obsession and fascination with consciousness. Sadly, though this was not my only experience with surrender – clearly, I hadn't understood the message it encompassed at that time. Of course Helen's ego knows best and continued to dominate, resulting in many more surrender experiences to come. You can see why daily surrender is now a necessity.

So, following that experience, I went on my merry way creating a life and stepping into finding and developing tools for me to help others while unwittingly still living out similar patterns. But the outer landscape and how I executed that way of life looked different, so somehow that fooled me into thinking I was ok. How wrong I was. This shows precisely how the ego is very baffling.

I want to just mention here about the messages that filter through to us from the source much of the time. Most of us are so unaware of the significance of the messages, and it seems absurd to think that they would be such simple messages too. When we are locked in mentally, we hold beliefs that everything has to be so complicated from the ego's perspective. And that is certainly what I believed for pretty much forever.

I remember being introduced to a concept of god through Sunday school and I believe it was there that I identified that what I felt did not match with what I was being told. What I was hearing just made little sense to me: how could something separate and outside of me govern me, mostly through fear? I found this very odd. That only helped my disconnection rather than connecting.

I now know that beliefs are something I have the power to choose. Once I can establish and see what current belief I hold and how it is impacting my life, I can then choose differently and reach for a tool that will assist me in letting go of that old non-serving belief. I choose to see abundance all around me today. I choose to see the joy and love all around me and be the witness to other people's shadows and send only love without being drawn in. My heart wants me to know it is ok and safe to be open.

I have spent my whole life unconsciously putting people in roles outside of me via my ego to serve in validating my very being. This showed me my ability to not only doubt myself, but more importantly to show me how I can actually trust the inner wisdom and guidance that I have always had within my heart. I just needed to remember that.

So here I am, now in my forties, having gone through a process again to recalibrate my spiritual connection. I had previously walked away from a spiritual practice that ultimately saved my life and thought I can live and run my life all on my own, with no form of connection. I was totally misguided again in my thinking. My life had been a series of car crashes when I had tried to run the show from my ego perspective. This time around it has been about integrating the ego into my very being and not battling against it. The fact is, we all have an ego. We base it on a lower level of consciousness, which is mostly victim consciousness, that has held us in it for generations. But now is the time to transcend the ego from a loving consciousness, found in the heart and embrace the ego like a child. It needs to be held and reassured. When the ego is ignored, it shouts louder.

The ego has played a huge role in the collective consciousness and how we see the world today. So we are seeing the world rapidly break down and going through a transformation as we are entering higher levels of consciousness. This will only allow us to create and be in a beautiful heart-based reality on our planet.

As I mentioned before, the sense of having a mission in this life was at times an overwhelming feeling. It has governed my entire life, and I now know it to be true. However, there was always a hole to fill in my soul, which is what I know is the integration work I do now. Having that hole in my soul is where my ego took over. I studied and studied, serving only my intellectual self, feeding the belief that if I know more intellectually about spirituality, I will be ok and safe in this life and armed with the tools to protect me. Again I was separated from the one thing that would protect me and give me the feelings of safety and security, which is god consciousness. And where do I find that? Through surrendering the ego.

I began a newer version of spiritual practice after 43 years of my life when I had, yet again, held the thought that I was in the driving seat, and of course I know best. Which is clearly not true, the god source I am aligned to knows better. I made the choice to go back to follow a 12-step programme. It is important to emphasise that the 12 steps are a spiritual programme, not a religious one.

I want to state here that when I talk about the ego, I have learned to talk about it with love and not something to hate or run from as I had for such a long time. The ego is the part of me that just wants to be integrated into my whole being, while being nurtured and understood or perhaps accepted. The more I separate myself from it, the more it wants to be in charge and shouts loud. When we look at our collective consciousness during an experience of a pandemic that has brought us to this point in history, we can see how it has been one giant ego running around in a flap, trying to control the entire show, mostly through fear.

Most of our imprinting comes from our parents. They lived from a place of victim consciousness, which wasn't their fault, as they were oblivious to it. So when we work with the ego we have to realise that this is not about blame any more, it is more about having the awareness of what we need to understand and where these patterns came from. And then we need to forgive whilst remembering to forgive ourselves.

I'll be honest with you, as you go through an ego death it can be quite daunting. This is why it is essential to have a strong support network when you go through these experiences. The experiences you can have will be unfamiliar to you and potentially feel like you have nothing to cling onto any more. But at that point you are opening up to the unknown, and this is where pure creation lives. In the unknown you begin to be fully present in the creative force that you are and can fully emerge as who and what you really are.

The power of surrender is experienced in the heart space. It is not an intellectual process. It is a powerful energy to be felt. The paradox is that one feels the heart break but actually it is opening like a beautiful flower emerging in the spring time. It is a rebirthing from the darkness of the womb or creation, and out of the darkness comes the light and the beauty in us all. One has to surrender the will of the ego to emerge fully in the presence of love. Love is god or what your understanding of god is.

When we are in thinking, we are mostly in the past or future, and this can become a mental addiction that has imprisoned you. And it continues to imprison humanity within a distracted internal dream state, a kind of matrix which is reflected outwardly as ongoing planetary conflict, chaos and confusion. Now is the time to spend more time in 'nothing time'. In order to do that we must FEEL. Go into your heart where you will experience felt perception, presence.

As the months went by writing this book, the surrenders came thick and fast to me – some were big and some were little experiences. My intellectual self, as always, wanted to analyse why they were the length of time they were. Actually, this was irrelevant. It was just that level of consciousness was automatically programmed to look through the linear perspective of time. The higher part of me knew that there is no time to measure them against anyway, they were all just moments.

So once I surrender the ego and exist in a moment of the unknown, the important question is, who am I now? This was to be revealed to me more and more throughout my awakening journey.

Journal

List some of your current beliefs about yourself and about the world you live in.

Do the beliefs you have listed feel empowering?

Did you know you have the ability to change your beliefs?

Write in your journal what it FEELS like to read that YOU have the ability to change your beliefs.

What you believe you will begin to see in your outside world.

What is your ego shouting at you about right now?

Perhaps take a minute to write down what your ego has been constantly chatting away about, notice where you have been overthinking or your thinking is going around in a loop.

Be fearless and honest with what you write down.

CHAPTER 5

Ask

When you ask, you will receive

Asking. Hmmm, is this something you are familiar with? Or are you more familiar with just being told and have forgotten that you can actually ask? I shut down the ability to ask when I was a small child, mainly because I was told to stop asking why or be quiet. There was a firm belief then that children should be seen and not heard. I am sure this is something that you are familiar with. So with these disempowering experiences, I learned to not ask. Instead, I learned to constantly seek.

An addiction to opiates brought me to my knees for my second big surrender. At the time, I was being prescribed opiates by my doctors for a back problem. I now know, but didn't realise then, that I suffer with the disease of addiction. I could not stop taking them on my own accord and they were literally killing me. In the process of this surrender I felt like I had a week left to live, at most, before something detrimental was going to happen to me. And this time I would not come back from the edge.

This surrender experience found me falling to my knees and asking out loud for somebody to help me. The following day a higher power or god put someone from my past on to my path. Although I was asking out loud, I was somehow setting an intention and showing a willingness for something or someone to help me. That must have been the energetic vibration I was putting out. I had not seen the person who came back into my life that day for a very long time. It just so happened he knew how to help me and this was nothing short of a miracle in my opinion.

In that moment, it set me on a new trajectory in my life. I embarked on a detox. This meant being completely honest in order to draw on all the support necessary. I embarked on a programme of recovery, using a 12-step approach, which ultimately saved and transformed my life. Funny how this is a spiritual programme, yet again highlighting the power of our own spirituality. But please do not get this confused with religion.

So, to reinforce the power of asking here, had I not asked with the unquestionable force and ultimate surrender, I would have potentially gone on another pathway. I may not have had the opportunity to sit and write these words for you – and for myself. I stepped into an alignment immediately with a higher force running through me, which now guides me daily.

During this phase of my life I appeared to function from an outsider's perspective, but inside I was totally broken. There was a continuous hole in my soul. I had a good job; I was in a relationship, albeit a frequently volatile one. That was down to patterns playing out, but like I said earlier, the patterns can be the same but the details look different or the actors and the play look different.

Asking can also be quite an unconscious process. Although I wasn't actively asking anything day to day, it didn't mean that another part of my consciousness wasn't asking. I just was not aware of it. What I mean by that is I could be having unconscious thoughts asking for knowledge or information about something in my life, and then I begin to have an experience. Again I am totally unaware of the reasons why I am having this experience, when actually I have called that in. This is manifestation at play here, and we'll talk more about this later. We manifest all the time, but just not always consciously.

When you ask a question, you will invariably get an answer. Let go of the expectation that the answer will come there and then because it can show up in a way you least expected. And so it is important to keep an open mind. When the answer does come, are you aware enough to witness the answer and willing enough to see it when it smacks you in the face? Therefore, it's imperative to do the inner work to expand your awareness, so you can be present when the answer shows up. Perhaps when your ego is in resistance, this could be an opportunity to reflect on the intentions you have previously set, and questions you have put out to the universe. What are you resisting and why? Remembering the ego serves only to keep you safe and stuck.

I set out on a monumental journey of awakening in 2014, and I found myself asking a lot of conscious and unconscious questions. At this particular time I was going through a marriage break up and was numbing myself, again, with alcohol and codeine (an opiate). I was in the midst of suffering with depression, post-traumatic stress disorder known as PTSD, and severe anxiety. I did not know what the hell to do. All I knew was that my life needed to change significantly, and I surrendered fully to a guidance within me to support me and my daughter.

I believe I find myself in these moments of surrender because I have continuously asked god to show me and guide me, whether that be consciously or unconsciously. I have had such difficulty with the word god because of so much prejudice around it, but on reflection it always seems to be my go to, when 'the shit hits the fan' and I am out of ideas as to what to do.

Take a moment here to look at your own life. Is this true for you? When I use the word god, I am referring to the universe, the energy of everything.

I thought I held a lot of shame and embarrassment around believing in god. Actually, it was shame and embarrassment around using the word god. It was the fear and the ridicule I imagined I would endure, or the feeling of being under attack because of what I believe to be true. This goes very deep energetically when you look at old lives lived, if you believe in past lives where these experiences have played out before, particularly for healers, shamans and witches, etc.

When I intentionally ask, I allow myself to become aligned with the energy vibration that will manifest my experience. As the saying goes, be careful what you wish for. So first there is a desire and then there is an energy of intention which is found in the asking.

When I surrendered in those pivotal moments I had nothing left, I was empty inside and so this created a space and a desire could then rise up in me. Here, it was freedom from drugs. I entered a state of intention and was willing to let go of everything I thought I had control of and ask for help. I could not do life alone and on my terms, it just wasn't working AGAIN. I have noticed that before I get to that point of surrender, I am completely running on my own self-will.

I say a little prayer every morning now with the energy of intention from my heart so that I may hand over my will and allow myself to be guided. This is always, and perhaps always will be, a work in progress. The way I do my prayers is simply to go into the heart space and ask how I may be of service today to others. I'm not praying for my own needs as I know they will be taken care of as I hand my will over to a higher power.

By 2017, more of me was unravelling, and I was given a step-by-step guide to follow. This information came through following a meditation and was yet another example of listening to my own guidance. And it couldn't have been more accurate for what I needed at that particular point in time. It shows how it didn't come from my thinking in my head, but more from my heart. My thinking would always distort it.

Here is the step-by-step guidance I was given:

1. Be honest with yourself

2. Love your dearest

3. Watch and learn

4. Read, read and then read some more

5. Write down all that comes to you – EVERYTHING

6. Witness teachings

7. Parent wholeness and presence

8. Trust yourself!!!

9. Regularly go within

10. Protect the foundation of you

11. Be strong and grounded

12. Be

It sure has been a ride!

I was taken aback when I received that guidance because it made so much sense to me on every level. I was up in my head being driven by constant programming. I could not see the simplicity of life and what was necessary at that moment in time.

It was during this time in 2017 that I remember still asking myself, who am I? After asking, I found the answers that usually come are a lot simpler than anything my complicated ego would come up with.

When I stop asking, I find myself shutting down and disconnecting from my higher self.

I've noticed that this lack of asking for help or guidance is common in older generations, because of the conditioning of attitudes of the 'stiff upper lip', this is just how it is and we mustn't show weakness.

Again, take a moment here and ask yourself: what would it feel like to fully trust in yourself? What would it mean for you to trust the inner guidance, the feelings, the intuitive nudges and not so much the inner narrative in your head? Especially if it has nothing nice to say about you. True inner guidance comes from a higher level of consciousness and is only loving, nurturing and supportive. Destructive thought patterns come from victim consciousness that many have been in for so long without even realising it because it has been the norm in society.

Many of us are conditioned to not think outside of the box or think for ourselves, believing that we should sit and wait to be told what to do, even if it makes no sense at all. In this state of thinking, we lose the ability to see sense in ridiculous systems or models that we believe we should all be conditioned to conform to. This negates our very core essence, which is fundamentally driven by love.

As there is no separation, our higher self really works through others. So if we stop asking the questions: the why, the how, the where and so on, then the answers cannot show up for us.

Question everything. Go ahead and Ask.

Allow yourself to go deeper and ask yourself – Who am I? And it will amaze you what it reveals to you.

Journal

Go ahead and ask yourself the question Who am I? There is always an answer to come, even if it happens to be I don't know. This is common when this question is asked. We often THINK we know who we are, but it is not always the truth of who we are.

I'd love you to take some time here to perhaps work through your own beliefs and prejudices around the word god.

How often do you ask for help or guidance within yourself or even from others?

How often have you witnessed others afraid to ask for help or guidance? Perhaps this has been you?

Is asking for help seen as a sign of weakness?

What is your experience of this?

Again, take a moment here and ask yourself: what would it feel like to fully trust in your inner guidance system? The feelings, the intuitive nudges, and not so much the inner narrative in your head?

CHAPTER 6

Let Go

Embodying love

What is the first thing that pops into your mind when I say the words 'let go'? When I used to hear this from other people, usually accompanied by care and kindness, I would spiral into more frustration. Why? After all, they meant well. It was because it appeared that other people could just let go of stuff and I didn't know how to. It was the 'how' of letting go that always puzzled me. I also didn't know what the hell I was actually supposed to be letting go of. What was essential for me to let go of was the beliefs I held that kept me locked into patterns that kept reoccurring in my life.

Letting go is not a simple task for someone who has an obsessional mind, especially when you don't even have the awareness of having an obsessional mind. Now I have that awareness of how my brain functions and the tools to help with that, but this was not the case for me growing up or in early adult life. Now I understand how this links to my battles with addiction and other labels of ADHD, ADD. Many people unknowingly suffer with addiction to thinking, because it appears to be such a normal part of life, but causes so much suffering.

Let's be clear about what I mean when I say, 'to let go'. In this context I mean to let go of the conditioned self, the ego programmes, the mask, to really allow in the only power that is there to serve everything. That power is love or the vibrational energy of love.

Sounds easier said than done, doesn't it? I know it isn't easy when you are totally locked into your thinking. To let go is to transcend the ego identity which is made up of the incessant programmes and patterns playing in our minds.

This is also an opportunity for surrendering judgement. I found I was constantly in judgement of myself and then judging others, but not maliciously, more comparatively. Have you noticed how much you judge yourself? By letting go of judgement and surrendering, you can step into a space of witnessing. Be the witness to what arises within, judging none of it, only giving it love. After all, we are all one collective consciousness, so what you judge in others you judge in yourself. Let go of the need to judge.

As I practice surrender, my humble heart breaks open and is immediately flooded with love within the silence and simplicity of that moment. I can then feel the divine love envelop me and I have proven this to be my only solution to everything. As I let go and open myself up to higher guidance within my heart, I can make better and more informed choices.

Time and time again I allow myself to fully let go through surrendering and allow love to open up my heart and break open those barricades. I have to be honest here, this is still a work in progress. This is because I have a default setting that is so strong that it will put on that protective mask again and barricade my heart in until the time comes to surrender once more. This allows me to feel a deeper level of love within me. So when I talk about love I am referring to everything, creation, the divine or god. Choose whatever word you feel more comfortable with.

In this book I've told you mostly about the bigger, lifesaving surrenders. However I find myself surrendering most days, it has become a huge part of my life. And it certainly makes life much more pleasurable.

During the summer of 2020, I had an experience of surrender before I was due to do an energy session with a client. I totally opened myself up and put down the false self, the mask, in order to be the conduit for the energy to come through for them. I really did not expect to feel the level of divine love I did in that particular moment. It was so divine that I cannot attach words to it because at that level of the divine, there are no words. The feeling I had brought me to tears. As the tears flowed, I felt a complete love and a knowing that it held me in a place of safety and security that was so undeniable; I knew it was ok to totally let go. This experience reminded me of a time a few years ago when I journaled some words from my guides after meditating and saw how I was now channelling from the energy of love. There are no words that will match that energy vibration because it is a felt perception.

One of my greatest desires has always been to fill my life with love and allow myself to experience love fully in my heart again. And to feel it without having to attach a label or a condition to it. This is not an effortless task if you are looking at it from a mental perspective of how you believe love is meant to be and is usually overshadowed with conditions.

I had spent my whole life just wanting to be able to feel again. But actually what I really wanted to feel was that divine essence of who I am, love. My heart had been barricaded in for such a long time, and evidently the journey for me has been to come back to love. The desire was always there, but I was not always conscious of it and, like many, I projected that role onto someone else to provide me with that love. That was always going to be difficult to receive when my heart was barricaded with conditions and limitations.

Now at age 45 and having recently had another big surrender and realisation, I am living connected to a power much greater than me. I can trust that this power within me is guiding me for the highest good of all humankind, not just myself, because when I view it as myself, I am in separation. Through my surrenders I can morph myself into the Oneness of all, and I know that by telling you this my words are coming from a place that can only be used to serve. Service is my greatest desire, especially during this monumental time of awakening consciousness.

We are in a period of making history. It's time to really embody the level of consciousness that is love, as a collective, to make manifest the world we want to see. Letting go of all the old within you that is no longer serving that vision is essential right now, and that takes integration work. It is our thinking that serves to separate us further and at the moment we are faced with so much messaging and media continuing to promote that separation. As I continue to say, it's time to question everything, and it's certainly a practice I instill into my daughter – to question everything. My desire is to raise a child that is a freethinker, without impressing too much of my unconscious patterning onto her. I am not perfect by any means, but to just have the intention to raise her to be a sovereign being allows me to step further into my sovereignty and be fully guided while letting go of all that does not serve that.

As I continued to let go or perhaps better explained as a shedding of the conditioned and programmed self as a daily practice, I realised it was time to get to know the real me, my true essence and parent myself through the getting to know me process. Once I let go, a new and true identity could emerge. I could gain some acceptance around my continuous journey of awakening to higher levels of consciousness.

So what did I need to let go of? EVERYTHING I thought I knew. What do I continuously need to let go of daily? EVERYTHING, in order to continuously be open to other perspectives that I don't need to attach myself to. I just need to be aware of them. This is how we access other dimensions which as energy beings, we are all capable of. This has not been a straightforward task for me, but it is totally possible. For me it takes continuous surrender, but as I say, it is a constant practice and I am nowhere near perfect at it. But I get to a point of being so uncomfortable within myself that the only solution is to surrender and transcend the ego self.

It seems insane, which I suppose it is, that after all the powerful spiritual experiences I have been blessed with, my ego likes to convince me they are not true and actually I cannot live my life from that standpoint. That is false: I absolutely can, and that belief resonates with everything I believed as a young child, always questioning the structures and systems that I was told to live by. That really did not make sense to me then. It's time to let go of those systems and structures to build new ones from a heart-based place and higher consciousness. We are seeing this now in the world. Like the ego, it has to collapse to rebuild a new identity. We are truly seeing an opportunity in the world now, the transition into a fresh way of being and living that serves all humankind, not just the few. As I step into the presence of love within my heart, I am able to access the true wisdom, higher wisdom, intuitive guidance, all with the vibration of love. Within that space there are no limiting beliefs, repeated patterns, programmed thoughts. There is only stillness, silence, presence, simplicity and true intelligence. As I constantly surrender, I am faced with this truth and evidence.

Silence and simplicity are key. It reminds me of a song that most resonates with my core and did so when I first heard it back in my twenties after my first rock bottom. The song was 'Silence' by Sarah McLachlan. This song touched my soul and after looking at the lyrics, I could see why. Again, it's only now that those words are so powerful to me and make so much sense for who and what I am today. I urge you to find it and listen to it.

I crave the silence from the mental noise within me and from the outside world. Through the art of surrender and meditation, I can connect with the silence. For so long in my life I knew no other way other than to escape through substances and self-medicating, momentarily giving me release, but that would only lead to my demise. Self-medicating can be any form of distraction that allows you to lose yourself. Currently, the easy availability of the media has a way of doing that. Let's face it, addiction to phones and media is common for most people. The key problem with that form of distraction is that it is often reinforcing hidden programmes and beliefs that may well be provoking fear within you.

I got to a point where I didn't want to just continue to read about spirituality in books. I had done that for most of my life because it was my passion. I wanted to experience the divine and be the one to write about those experiences. But first I had to let go of everything within me that blocked that process. And as I did, so I began the writing process once and for all.

As I wrote this book, I had such a strong feeling of love in my heart. Tears rolled down my face with a knowing in my heart that I can finally feel safe. I could trust in the process and the journey I am on to integrating and embodying the real me, but first I had to let go and continue to let go through the art of surrender.

There are many tools and methods that can be used for healing and connecting, and over the years I have tried and used most of them. But in my experience, sometimes they became more of a blocker and a mechanical process because I could not get out of being in my head. I needed to access a higher consciousness first, which has only come to me through surrender. Once I surrendered, I could then really utilise those tools for any energetic healing that I needed. Having surrendered, I could access my connection to the heart.

As I threw myself into training, it was clear that I was gathering more knowledge intellectually, which was all very interesting, but for me there was a vital component missing. This missing part was the fundamental intention for connection to take place and still a lack of belief that there was actually something far more powerful, beyond the mind that could reconnect in my heart. I still had a lot of self-doubt in my own abilities and still wasn't trusting, despite having a knowing at such a young age. But that knowing had been pushed to the side as I had no one to nurture that part of me. This is one reason I am so passionate about how we can really nurture our children today. I believe that those who have different disorders and being drugged so routinely are perhaps being labelled unnecessarily.

The information I received from my last surrender was that no matter how much I look externally for where I might fit in and what label I put on myself, I will never find it. This alone stands in the way of me just showing up. It prevents me taking the role of spiritual teacher that god has very clearly assigned to me by delivering many opportunities to surrender, and to hear this guidance, which gets louder and louder each time.

The lifelong question I have asked is: what is my purpose? What am I doing here? This a question asked by many of us – perhaps you too? The very simple answer was self realisation and to serve others by connecting to the divine, the director of my life. I cannot begin to tell you the battle I have had with this because I now cannot avoid the word GOD. And to be honest with you, I don't feel the need to any more.

The word held so many negative beliefs. I was a work in progress undoing those beliefs alone, but the fact of the matter is that I now sense that there isn't any part of me that does not embody that word and everything that goes with my understanding of the word GOD. The questions that immediately come to me are: what do I do with the true knowing, not the intellectual knowing, but the divine knowing? And how do I integrate that into my life? It's important here to remind you and myself that by letting go, I let go of the outcome and the 'hows' of how the divine should show up in my life. If I hold on to the 'hows' my ego begins to try to run the show again.

I held on to so much shame and embarrassment for allowing myself to believe in the divine or god and actually wanting to do god's work. When I think about it, all I have ever really wanted to be is a spiritual teacher. It's always been the only thing that lights me up, lights that spark within me, the god spark. I battled with the fact that I wanted to be a spiritual teacher for such a long time, in fear of being ridiculed and labelled as some crazy god freak, when actually they were all just self-imposed beliefs. Those beliefs served to keep me small and insignificant and keep me isolated from others, when in fact, the opposite of that is what serves us. It's connection.

One belief I held was that if I came out as believing in a god or the universe, I wouldn't have any friends or my partner would think I was some weirdo and I would end up all alone and lost. But then that is how I felt anyway when I was disconnected from the universal love. I am such a control freak when I am up in my head; I have to be able to control what I do with god. How hilarious is that? My daily practice is to get me out of the way so god can guide me to be of service, be the vessel for the universe to flow through me and be what I was sent here to be. I do not follow any particular religion and in all honesty have avoided religion because I find it so conditioned and controlling. My understanding of spirituality is of connecting with source energy or god.

Again, my greatest desire was to be a channel, and I constantly kept missing the fact that I was already doing it. Desire is when you tap into your highest soul path, despite not understanding it logically. I kept looking at and slipping into comparing myself with how other people channelled the spiritual path, for example, as working with spirits, etc. It was through my words and writing that I was acting as a channel and also how I connected in with my energy sessions with people. Boy, did it take me ages to realise that!

We are all natural channels; it is not special to one person. It's a case of fully understanding that you too have access to higher wisdom that is ready to come through and be expressed within your very core.

Using the word channel for ease, the channelled writing really began for me more intensely in 2014. I had written quite a lot in my early 20s, but I had disregarded it and stopped. Looking back now it was an accurate representation of my self-doubt, although what I had written then was totally relevant for today's world. I used to write about the ego self, living in the present moment and have lots of experiences through meditation, but I doubted it.

I want to share with you how letting go I am able to receive guidance and tap into it through meditation and journalling. This is a lifesaver and a process of trusting too. I hope this is useful for you.

Letting go allows me to follow my heart's intelligence, the inner GPS system. Here I'd like to share with you some of the profound messages I received at a difficult time in my life, how those messages came about and why I now follow what I receive wholeheartedly.

CHANNELLING

In 2014, I began the journey of a tremendous change in my world. This included a separation from my relationship at the time and a complete breakdown of my personal world as I knew it. My daughter was 2 years old at that time. One evening I felt the 'nudge' through persistent thoughts to pick up a pen and paper. The thoughts were different to my normal thought – like words, but with a different resonance to them. I was used to the words that were self-destructing at that point, so that is how I knew the difference. Being the stubbornly strong-willed individual I can be, I eventually succumbed to the persistent instruction, and picked up the pen and paper to write. And it just flowed out of me, with no time for me to analyse what the words were until my hand stopped writing. When I looked back at it, it was with disbelief, if I am honest.

The words that flowed were:

You are about to embark on a mammoth journey of enlightenment and accreditation. In order to be ready for this journey you need to purify yourself and how you will do this is to follow everything we guide you to do. You ask who we are but you are not to know right now because if you know it will hinder your progress and that is not what we wish for you. You will need to see clearly with the process and you will need strength. How you acquire that strength is by trusting us as we guide you. Help is always at hand whenever you need it, you simply need to ask.

What is in store for you is now your life's mission and it is very important that you follow this, do not allow anyone or anything to stand in your path and do not be swayed by physical desires as you are being now (referring to my battle with addictions).

What we ask of you will only enrich your life. Please do not hold back or be frightened, we have been waiting patiently for this moment so just trust.

At this point my consciousness was asking a question as to who the hell was talking to me and the answer that came was:

Yes, we are us, a collective.

I now believe this to be the collective consciousness of the children. I, like many lightworkers, am here to be a guardian for the children in these tumultuous times.

The overwhelming feeling and word that stood out was TRUST. Not a simple thing to do when you have spent your life being a control freak.

The words continued to flow:

> *How you go about things is unique to*
> *you and no other will encounter this so*
> *just do and move forward with trust and*
> *curiosity, we will keep you safe. Allow*
> *others to guide you and feel enriched*
> *by their generosity, do not be afraid.*
> *When you get that urge to write, we*
> *will communicate, FEEL IT, allow us to*
> *move through you, embrace your gift.*

Wowzers is what I thought when I read it back! While I was writing it, there was no time to stop the flow and read it or analyse the words. It came out so quickly. I remember thinking to myself, is there actually truth around what I am now writing? Where the hell is this information coming from? And what do I do with it? Can I actually trust what it is saying to me? When I wrote this, I was at a massive turning point in my life. As I said, I had decided to walk away from a toxic relationship and I had a two-year-old daughter. The messages I was getting in my consciousness were so loud that I had to step into the unknown, not knowing how the hell my life was going to turn out. It was clearly the beginning of another transition for me.

This channelled information was just the beginning of more information that was to come through, but looking back now I can see that I was just being an open channel even when I wasn't writing, I just didn't realise it. I was too busy looking at others doing work that I knew I was destined to do, but I clearly needed a lot more unravelling and my time would emerge. This time is now, and this book is a part of it.

A few years passed by after writing that first piece of channelled information before I went on to write anything more of significance. During those years I allowed myself to be completely guided during a very difficult phase of unravelling, which included treatment for PTSD and depression. My focus was to be the best mother I could be during my unravelling, and knowing that if I listened fully to my guidance, I could be the mother that my daughter was guiding me to be. I let go and trusted.

As I unravelled my conditioned self, it showed my true identity.

Journal

What do you currently believe love to be in your life?

Are you totally fulfilled from the inside? Or are you seeking outside of yourself first for love?

What do you believe is your purpose? Is this a question you have often asked?

Go ahead and free-write some words that come after asking yourself these questions.

What would it feel like to you to tap into and trust the divine wisdom that comes through you?

How different would your life potentially look with that inner wisdom?

CHAPTER 7

Identity

The abyss of identity
The great space

Abyss means an immeasurably deep gulf or great space.
And some definitions of identity are:

- *the distinguishing character or personality of an individual: INDIVIDUALITY*

- *sameness in all that constitutes the objective reality of a thing: ONENESS*

So, from asking 'Who am I?' I went through a process of letting go. The old me from an ego perspective was completely broken to pieces. The structures in my mind were completely dismantled, and they left me with a feeling of the complete unknown.

In 2017 I started to have experiences after standing in front of the mirror and looking directly into my own eyes and asking, 'Who am I?'

As I went through the breakdown of my conditioned identity, I had some very strange experiences during the night when I woke up. As I awoke from sleep, I would experience complete blankness and just awareness and being in that moment. It would take what felt like a few minutes for the mind to generate thoughts to remind me of who I was. During these experiences I realised more and more the power that my thoughts had to convince me of who I thought I was from the programming in my mind. I was aware of the conditioned programming, like computer software, running through my head and grasped at the identity of the Helen I was familiar with.

This was a very odd experience to begin with, but I began to get used to it over time. I allowed myself to merge more with the nothingness of pure creation and pure essence.

My biggest awakening experience began in 2014, as I mentioned earlier. Around this time, I had experiences during the night that would wake me up in a bit of a panic. They appeared to be dreams that held number sequences in them. I later realised that these number sequences related to energetic changes that I was going through. I'll be honest with you, though – it freaked me out. It felt like they related it to my energetic connection to my daughter. If I didn't input the correct number sequence in my dream, then I would lose the connection to my daughter. This is why I woke up in a panic. As the years went by, the dream evolved into being more about my connection with my higher being and my true identity that was very clearly being upgraded and integrated. The more deeply I delved into my energetic work, especially at the level of understanding the nature of DNA structuring and consciousness, the more I realised the actual nature of this experience. Energetic work is often like putting pieces of a puzzle together.

Some of the reasons I used to wake up in a panic during the night was because I felt like parts of my consciousness was being taken somewhere and parts were not coming back as I woke. I now realise that this was part of higher aspects of my soul fully integrating and leaving behind the old parts of me that were essentially dying.

Then again, in 2017 I had many experiences during the night. I remember waking up and writing the words 'the abyss of identity'.

What did that term mean? At the time I could only relate it to the depths that my tortuous false identity repeatedly took me to, which at times was like hell. The depressions were like a bottomless pit – like an abyss.

My patterning and programming only served to destroy me. I had a head that was out to kill me – it had nothing good to say about me but it consumed me. It had become my identity, constantly going round in a loop of repeated patterns until I surrendered again. I heard my spirit say to me that it was time to level up. This prompted me to take physical action to embody a spiritual solution. I had clearly experienced the number sequences as a DNA restructuring in order for me to now surrender the old me, in order to step fully into the new me.

I made the conscious choice to level up, by putting down the substances again that were suppressing me and keeping me numb. I embarked on the 12-step programme again, which today is my foundation. Had I not really listened to that inner voice in 2019, I would have remained on the path of self-destruction. This would have led to the end of me in this physical world. Perhaps at that point, though, it was the end of me, the old me, as I embarked on another level of waking up to who and what I really am. As the unravelling began, the transformation was rapid and truly miraculous.

Since 2019 I have continued to have many more 'mini surrenders'. A fairly recent one has been one of the most powerful surrenders I have ever experienced. That one allowed me to completely let go of my idea of how my life was supposed to look and, in essence, allow my ego and false identity to be smashed to pieces again. This revealed to me who and what I really am. The only part of me that was left in that moment of surrender was my desire to serve others and be a spiritual teacher in the new world, a spiritual teacher of the new paradigm. I could not fully step into this identity until I allowed my programmed and false identity that the ego had developed to be dismantled and create a great space to open up. This space allowed the higher part of my soul to fully integrate and be part of the whole and not be separate any more.

As my new identity emerged, it combined with the essence of creativity flowing with source or the quantum field and unfolding with manifesting. The old victim consciousness Helen, full of blame, self-pity, frustration, control, anger, hatred, self-destruction, disconnected from source and truth, finally disappeared in that moment. What it left was the immense desire for freedom and truth. And when truth shows itself, be ready – because it really does reveal itself.

New level consciousness Helen is compassionate, transparent, truth, love, free and able to live my life as a child of the universe, pure creation. I am back to my original blueprint that came into this world before the conditioning and before the labels. It is now safe for me to fully embody compassion and love without feeling disempowered by other people's views, opinions and perceptions.

Falling to my knees with these surrenders often resulted in my pride being hurt and some shame being stirred up in me. This was because I had allowed myself to get to that point – yet again. I was meant to be a spiritual person, or so I would always tell myself, but then that was my ego speaking to me. Now I was about to find out what being spiritual actually was – not the ego perspective of being spiritual. The amount of times I would say, and I would hear others say, 'I am a spiritual person'. Most could not define or describe what that actually means – I know I couldn't until I began to have these experiences. Being a spiritual person is not about me! When the 'me' is involved, then there is the spiritual ego. I can think and say to myself as much as I like I am a spiritual person. I can sit with my incense and candles as much as I like, but that does not make me a spiritual person. My spiritual ego can still pinpoint blame and point to others who lack spirituality. So what is spirituality? I would say it is CONNECTION.

NEW IDENTITY

One day as I was working on this book I heard loud and clear in my awareness, 'Helen, you are a spiritual teacher first and foremost.' That moment left me with two choices: I can either really accept this gift OR I can continue to search for something I will never find, because I already have it. I realised at that point that I have been a spiritual seeker my whole life. It's now time to let go of being the seeker and be the teacher. There is no better way to learn than to teach. The recent experience of stepping fully into the unknown on every level finally made complete sense.

The old me had to die for me to experience the new paradigm of consciousness running through every part of me, my new identity. A unified identity with all.

As I mentioned before, I had always had a desire to do divine work but feared being ridiculed or labelled a bible basher because I did god's work. This comes from my early years of feeling torn between wanting to be one of the cool kids and being seen, and following my natural instincts to protect and look out for those that got picked on. I was torn between different worlds of experience. If I were one of the cool kids everything would be ok and I would feel accepted, heard and seen. And oh boy, was I seen for attempting to be one of the cool kids. If you want to talk about being rebellious or maybe misguided, I could tell you a thing or two! I believe that a rebellious streak serves us when we are being misguided, especially now in times of information overload and misinformation being fed to our minds.

My true source connection and deep desire to connect with my true self was hidden in the guise of a spiritual ego, and I came to realise this as I wrote this book. It's like another cloud that keeps you in the shadows and controlled by still having the ability to judge and compare. This judgement and comparison of yourself and others is not with any ill intention but mostly to keep you under the illusion that you will be safe. It just keeps you small spiritually. The many smoke screens that the spiritual ego can throw up are things like I need to be more spiritual, I must prove to people that I am spiritual that way no one will hurt me, and people will like me. No one, including my 'self', will see the levels I go to, to self-destruct. Again, another bid to be recognised, acknowledged, to be seen for the inner truth that wants to unfold within me.

Many in today's society are in self-destruct mode and often totally unaware of it. Hiding behind consumerism, distraction from devices, substances, etc. Why? Because it is what we are conditioned to do. The only solution to this is to connect into the higher self and experience source energy again, that from which we came.

It is difficult to witness the truth in another when sitting in the spiritual ego. I cannot even see the truth I am from a spiritual ego. I needed only one spiritual teacher in my life and that is the divine and to be present in how the experience of the divine wanted to show up for me. This is where I experienced the paradigm shift in spiritual teachings and saw how we are our own gurus as sovereign beings. I have found a lot of the old spiritual teachings are quite fear-based and unconscious. Unless you can really see the smoke screen you are hiding behind in the guise of the spiritual ego, you can't let it go.

I can only share about spiritual experiences that have revolutionised my life and that have pretty much saved it every time. At last I was convinced through experience that a connection to source energy was the only solution for me. Being connected to source removes and relieves all of my perceived problems and issues.

My primary purpose on this planet is to experience the full magnitude of who and what I am and serve others. I do not need any labels to do that. I have spent my whole life under labels, whether by attaching them to myself or allowing others to do so. I am able to step into roles, but really I have no requirement for a label to define me or trap me into a false identity.

As you expand your own consciousness, which I highly recommend now, and tap into your own intuitive abilities, you will discover your own truth and natural soul path or purpose in life. Our ultimate purpose collectively is to step into our higher selves and collectively create a world where we get to experience the full magnitude of that which we are. Let go of the limited illusion of self, the control many people feel they need, and begin to witness the mechanisms that are used to control, especially on a mass scale.

I recently realised why I had always felt like I didn't fit in. It's because I couldn't fit the totality of who and what I actually was in the labelled space or role that was expected of me. There was a sense that something was missing, like a feeling of having a hole in my soul. In reality, it was because I could not be fully present in my body until the energetic vibration on the planet was that of the vibration of love. Remember, vibrations and frequencies are energy. This feeling is true for many highly energetically sensitive children and also many adults today. It is only recently that I feel that I have fully embodied my physical vessel. As I said before, you are an energy being first with a physical body.

You may resonate with the experience of not fitting the full magnitude of who and what you are into your vessel. This is certainly the case with the children in today's world. Their energy and consciousness is so vast that it is proving a challenge to continuously shape them to fit into outdated structures and systems via a means of control. Sadly, I believe this is why many are being labelled very quickly as having something wrong with them. How do we allow the magnificent energy to integrate into a small physical vessel? We allow it by adapting the systems to accommodate who and what they are. It's not about drugging children to fit into outdated systems. That clearly doesn't work any more.

I asked the question, 'How do we live a life without trying to fit our true identity into limiting and labelled boxes that often stop us living a fulfilled life?' As energy beings, we are a vast colour of frequencies that absolutely cannot be put into boxes. This only serves to separate and fragment us. The time is now to include every aspect of ourselves and to form spaces in society where that is at the forefront for living, where true creation can flourish.

Journal

What is your understanding of spirituality?

Does spirituality currently have a role in your life? If not, ask yourself why not.

How do you connect with your inner self?

Is there a particular practice you have thought about doing but haven't yet? What is stopping you?

CHAPTER 8

Surrender & Sovereignty

I hope by now you have seen how I have scattered the word 'surrender' throughout my writing and as I write it again, it only confirms to me that surrender is the ultimate starting point. After all, if you think about it, we are born into this world in a surrendered state of being, pure creation. The act of and the willingness to surrender completely opens up a channel within you to create anew. You are life; therefore, you are creation. If I am creation, then my child is creation and a sovereign being just as I am.

The experiences I have had over the last 18 months or so, which include the duration of writing this book and watching global events happening, have proven to me that we are sovereign. And because of old ways of thinking, we have been controlled and enslaved so much in our own thinking. These experiences and revelations have reformed my whole life. As I am part of a collective consciousness, I am beginning to see the revolution taking place not only within but also in the outside world. Remember – we are the creators, so what we hold in our consciousness we will create on the outside world.

I could no longer live within the confines of my destructive mind; I was ready to allow a new level of consciousness to emerge and to trust it. At this point in history we must remember our sovereignty and no longer allow ourselves to be the victims of what we see, hear and feel from the outside world. Remember, we are the creators, therefore what we want to see, hear and feel comes from within because we access that level of consciousness from there. Lessen the distractions and go within regularly and then act from a higher state of consciousness. As a great speaker of truth once said, the kingdom of heaven is within, so as we awaken and access that kingdom held within our own sacred hearts, we create heaven on earth. It's as simple as that. This has revolutionised my own life. True heart-centred living.

At the moment you surrender you open up a gateway for true knowing to flow in. When you are in that moment of stillness and silence you have the potential to have a realisation that there is no battle to be had, that is the illusion projected from the beliefs held in the mind.

You are safe and protected when you can allow yourself to access the pure intelligence of the heart, your source energy.

I can now surrender and access the truth within me. I can step into my own sovereignty, knowing that I am supported and guided at any moment. I only have to surrender myself to the higher consciousness that is there to serve for the highest good of all humanity. The new experiences I have had following my surrenders have provided the evidence I needed to know that it works. I only need to acknowledge that simplicity.

As I continuously look at the beliefs and thoughts that are playing around in my head, I am able to surrender them, let go of them with the aid of tools and techniques. I continue to hold the belief that the source energy that flows through me only wants to serve for the highest good and does not want to destroy. My previous self-destruction came from a lower level of consciousness held in my mind.

The art of using surrender is a continuous daily practice for me now, instead of waiting until I am beaten. I am allowing myself to be a work in progress. I realised I could use this beautiful practice at any moment I choose and I can enter a space within.

The intellectual part of me or the ego part of me does not have to be the one with all the answers to keep me safe as I can simply surrender to all that is and ask for the guidance needed that is going to serve the highest consciousness of all. I can then go forward from that vantage point, which usually presents the answers laced with simplicity. While I believe that I have to have all the answers to life, I am in the spiritual ego and not in the purity of consciousness that is ever-expanding within me. I have to let go of how those answers are going to come and what they should look like – that is not up to me. It is only the ego trying to govern and tell me how things are supposed to look.

As I continue daily to surrender to the universal intelligence running through my being, it is an upward spiral to step further into my own sovereignty. The only way for me to be fully sovereign is to open up and access the truth held within my heart's intelligence. We can all access that greater intelligence from within and it's totally ok to trust it.

As we begin to choose the path to trust, however, it can often throw up some conflict within. After all, most of us have lived a life with self-doubt and relied only upon fear-based instruction. As I wrote this book, it brought me more awareness of the massive increase and intensity of information overload via the media. This activates so many thought patterns, triggers and the potential to input new beliefs to hold that, perhaps, don't make sense. Much of this may not be serving for the greater good. It has given me a further opportunity to really practise discernment, be aware of what was really ringing true with me and also, how it was making me feel.

SURRENDERING THROUGH MISCARRIAGE

I would like to share another profound experience I had during my last big surrender, and that came through my last miscarriage. I have gone through four miscarriages and each one has been so different. Before I continue here, I want to take this opportunity to honour and give my love to every woman that is reading this book who has also experienced miscarriage. To me, miscarriage has always felt a difficult topic to openly share about. I chose to share some of my experience at the time I was going through my last miscarriage and I have made the choice to share it with you now as I don't believe that it should be a taboo subject. And if my daughter reads this book, I wish for her to feel empowered to fully express how she feels, should she go through the same experience.

As I was experiencing my last miscarriage, the overwhelming energetic message I was receiving into my conscious awareness felt like a new sort of transformation was taking place. It was one that I needed to fully express in order for me to process and become. It felt like I was going through a rebirthing for myself. The energy felt like a new level of consciousness had opened up within my very being. I knew I would not experience the physical manifestation of a child in the way I had imagined by creating and carrying another child full term. However, the energy that merged within me throughout the 10 weeks of carrying the developing foetus became a metamorphosis experience to create the opening for my creative presence and a new version of me to be born.

This miscarriage had been a totally different experience for me, and I am a different person to who I was before miscarriage. It may seem strange, but I was able to see many blessings and miracles while allowing myself to experience the heartbreak and loss, without feeling the need to go into my old self-pitying and self-destructive default settings. This was a miracle in itself and an example of the power of allowing. This time I made the conscious choice not to blame myself for not being able to carry a child and not to put myself into the consciousness of being a victim again. The level of consciousness that I was opening up to would not allow me to do that. This was most certainly the vibration of love. Remembering that I was stepping further into love, which has been my greatest desire, to come back to love.

The biggest transformational message I received in my experience of this miscarriage was that WOMEN ARE AMAZING AND ABSOLUTELY PHENOMENAL BEINGS. Hallelujah! I had finally united with the divine and sacred energy of the feminine, pure creation that I am, and I'm the only creation that needs to come true.

As I reflect on what was happening to me at that time with the pregnancy and miscarriage on an energetic level, I realised it was a deep healing experience of my past. It was ancestral healing and forgiveness on a deep level as I gave birth to me as a newer and higher consciousness.

The question I had at the time was around the fundamental intention of this pregnancy – was it ever meant to be about the possibility of birthing a child? Or was it about healing the deeper child within me to be able to give birth to me again? The answer that profoundly spoke loud and clear to me was the latter.

The other realisation I had with my miscarriage experience was that it was totally ok for me to accept and allow myself to be truly vulnerable. It was ok to allow people to hold, love and support me through all of what I felt. I did not need to be alone as I had often felt throughout my life, a feeling that came from feeling so alone and unsupported as a child. I want to really emphasise here to you that those feelings were no one's fault; it is just how these experiences have been passed down from our ancestors. By having these experiences, I could consciously choose to allow that programming to stop there and then. As I allowed myself to be fully immersed in my own healing, this opened up a channel for me to heal the past and all those that played a role in it. This in turn influences and transforms the future on an energetic level.

Huge paradigm shifts within me took place and there was no going back – the door had shut on my old identity.

My feeling is that humanity as a collective has spent too long existing in realities that only serve to separate us from each other and encourage us to look at our differences, rather than looking at what unites us and serves us for a higher purpose.

Freedom and sovereignty are your god-given right.
In 2012, a new level of consciousness was born as I gave birth to my daughter. A part of me knew it was time to embrace my own truth, finally. A part of me knew that the generational patterns had to stop, and it had to stop with me. As I went on the journey to reconnect with me, I could continuously connect with my daughter from a higher vibrational energy. This has allowed me to bring her up with an understanding of how important it is to experience everything about who she is, and how her being correlates to the 'is-ness' of everything in existence. This gives her the ability to tap into the one true source of everything and to trust in her own inner guidance system.

Surrender, connection, trusting and sovereignty.

SOVEREIGNTY

Sovereignty is self-governing.

We came into this world free, innocent and expressive, knowing only love. You have the freedom and choice to be that way, if only you allow yourself.

As we evolve as a human species, we understand and experience how we are complete sovereign beings that work in unity with each other, not against. We are here to reconnect with the intelligence that is within each and every one of our hearts, not in our heads – the hearts of ALL human beings, especially our children. Our children are sovereign beings just like us, and they are here to show us and remind us of our own sovereignty.

Nothing on the outside world can control you once you step fully into your sovereignty.

The more you open up to your heart and do the necessary clearing work on the inside of you, the more you free yourself from the chains that bound you. It is not up to anyone else to free you, it is you that has to free yourself from the shackles that are beliefs, whether they are imprinted or self-imposed. It's totally ok to look at the shadow aspects of yourself with love because that is how we neutralise and integrate them into our very being as we become whole again, just like we were at the moment of creation.

Change your beliefs, change your world.

Why is sovereignty paramount now? And what does it really mean?

If you are anything like me, the word 'sovereignty' was not used in my vocabulary, but it was a word that was echoing throughout my very being during my last surrender experience and as I began to write this book.

What the word 'sovereignty' means to me is about standing in my own power, my truth, embodying love and respecting other people's sovereignty, including my child's.

I, like many people, had been programmed to believe that we must be and do exactly what those we perceive to be in power tell us. We believe that we must do as they say because they must know best and must have our best interests at heart, surely. We must dance to their tune, but speaking from my experience, this seems to only lead to an inability to be responsible for our own lives. This only serves a consciousness that promotes a blame culture, which is the victim consciousness mentality that most are used to being in. It leaves us with feelings of powerlessness. And then we act from a place of fear.

We haven't come here as humankind solely to live from a place of fear, that is total disconnection from all that is. We came here to experience the magnitude of all that is and who and what we are. We came to live from a space of connection, love and joy, and be sovereign beings.

I am life and life is creation. I am, I am, I am.

I can create a world I want to see, and that comes from inside me.

The chemicals I spent most of my life consuming served only to give me a feeling of false security and safety and escape from my own self (the ego) so that I could experience some freedom, or reach oblivion because I found the density of this world too much. I searched for the freedom from self, the ego. But the impact of using those chemicals over time was killing my spirit.

I do not believe now that we need to be reliant on synthetic chemicals, many of which mostly alter our biochemistry. This is not freedom, nor is it sovereignty to me. This is continuous enslavement.

Life is living my truth as a sovereign being.

Journal

Some questions about Sovereignty for you to think about. Ask your heart the following questions and allow yourself to journal on your answers freely.

What does sovereignty mean to you?

How does it apply to you now?

How would being in your sovereignty change your world and the world at large?

And now some questions about Belief, your beliefs, to think about:

What beliefs are you questioning right now?

What beliefs are not in alignment with your core truth?

Are your beliefs disconnecting you or connecting you?

What beliefs are you happy to surrender now?

CHAPTER 9

Evolve

Truly living

A s I now have a daily practice of surrender, I allow myself to experience true abundance and gratitude with intention. What I mean by that is by making sure I am fully present in my practices and not just in the doing of it, for the sake of saying I have done it.

By surrendering first I am in the connected space of presence where the miracles begin to take place.

Ask yourself now what would it be like to finally truly live in accordance with the earth and co-create and step into your dreams? All it takes is to truly believe it is possible and you will see it. believe it is possible and then you will see it, as Wayne Dyer explains in his book *You'll See it When You Believe It*, rather than the other way around as is commonly heard, 'I'll believe it when I see it'.

A huge part of your own evolutionary process is to strip away all the self-limiting, self-imposed and programmed beliefs as I mentioned earlier. Then you start to get glimpses into what your soul's journey is on this planet and allow it to manifest into a reality for you. This is the reason for removing the old conditions and programmes you have running in your thought processes and that you are carrying in your energy field.

If you want to see someone with an expanded consciousness and connecting with all, free of any limited beliefs, then look at a young child or even your own child, or perhaps more importantly, in your own heart. All the answers are within your heart.

Co-create with the universe within and manifest from a surrendered and connected space within your heart.

Co-creating your reality comes from being totally aligned or coherent within your whole self. It comes from accessing the heart intelligence or god consciousness rather than trying to control reality and dictate how it should be according to your own thinking, which often is not aligned with higher consciousness thinking. As we let go of old beliefs and ways of thinking and step into the emotions of the heart, we can then consciously choose what we wish to think about in order to create. Now that is evolutionary.

You are a creative being – so get creative with the stories you are telling yourself. Are those stories serving you and humanity for the highest good? Or are they just limiting you?

We all have dreams in life, but who says that they have to stay dreams? Perhaps in your early years you were labelled a dreamer. The reason you have these ideas and dreams of the things you would love to do is because they are there to show you some direction that your life could potentially take. After all, there are infinite and immeasurable possibilities in the universe.

We all look at other people, such as so-called celebrities with fame and money, as if they have the most perfect life, and wish we could have that or other things to make us happy. Your happiness comes from within first. It comes from living the life you were born to live, not by living someone else's life. I was and still am always seen as the different one in my family.

I always held that inner knowing that all the current systems and structures that have been in place for so many years lacked the space to provide any freedom of expression and were simply not serving so many of us. I wanted to live my life freely and at times I did. Inevitably, given the disempowering beliefs I held for so long, I would often slip back into self-doubt and try to live the conditioned mainstream way of life. This way only impacted me negatively on a mental level, and I felt locked into myself and trapped. Because so many other people were comfortable living that way, it felt like I was expected to, which made me question my own intuitive beliefs – perhaps they were wrong? Now I know after many experiences with awakening that what I felt was correct for me. As I opened up and shared my experiences, I realised I was not alone. As I gave myself permission to be who I truly was and voice that, it gave permission for others to do the same. We share a commonality.

Truly living is to follow my own inner alignment and evolve. After all, that is what we are all here to experience, conscious evolution.

ABUNDANCE

We live in an abundant universe, it's as simple as that. When I mention the word 'abundance', does your mind instantly go to money or material possessions?

Money alone doesn't make you truly or 100% happy. I have always had money in some way and have always been able to manifest it, but it certainly did not bring me an abundance of happiness. Money has been the focus and drive in so many people's lives for such a long time and can be the source of so much corruption and manipulation too. Now I am not saying for one minute that I am against money because I am not. I have spent a long time looking at and continue to change the beliefs I hold around money. The form of currency we know as money is just one form of energetic exchange. It was important for me to reframe all of my old monetary beliefs in order for me to receive and use money in a way that was going to serve all for the highest good, and come from a totally aligned place within my heart.

Once we can reframe our beliefs about money, it opens up more experiences of abundance. Money comes and goes and flows like everything. I do not believe that it should be used for power and enslavement over others. This is corruption and is exactly how it has been and is being used now to enslave many people. During the pandemic we have seen this taking place. It is my belief that the darker aspects of this power are now coming to light to so many people as we awaken further. It's time the wealth was shared.

We all have a purpose in life and ultimately that is for your soul to express itself fully. We are here to connect and collaborate as a collective on this planet. You know when you're on the right track because everything flows with ease and grace without your thoughts getting in the way. Money, material things, support and opportunities will be presented to you if it is aligned with your soul essence.

Live with the belief that you are an abundant being because you are. Abundance is experienced in the moment.

As I mentioned enslavement earlier, take another moment to look at where your mind is enslaved. Are you truly living? Drug addiction is just one form of enslavement, which originates from thoughts. All forms of social messaging we see in the media, shopping, advertising, the list goes on... they all serve to enslave us. They only serve to suppress our core essence. They shut down our ability on a daily basis to see how we are already abundant. Perhaps all of those outside consumables are used just to aid further suppression of our emotional selves and result in enslavement more and more.

Truly living is releasing the slave within and stepping into true abundance and gratitude. This allows you to see outside the box that is filled with labels and the constant narrative of 'should', the constant doing. Just allow yourself to BE who you desire to be – allow yourself freedom and sovereignty.

I ask my heart daily, 'What will you have me be?' and it is at that point that I can enter the flow of simplicity, beauty and peace. The true simplicity of life filled with abundance on every level only to be found in the moment.

Living on purpose and living intentionally is key to co-creating with the universe. The energy of intention is so powerful.

You can become a blank slate at any moment you wish and choose again what you want to create. I now ask the heart intelligence rather than from my own distorted thinking. Choosing to truly live from the heart.

Thinking is a powerful tool for manifesting, and we have been blessed with a brain to use, to create. However, I believe we have been in a way of thinking that has not created the greatest outcomes for many for a long time until now. First, we must tap into the higher intelligence that is found in the heart and then use the brain for aligned thinking.

It's now time we allowed ourselves to evolve into the higher states of consciousness and create life on this planet that serves everyone and everything. It is the deepest desire within all of us, and especially our children. I look at the children with such awe because it's like they are waiting for us adults to wake up. They don't need to be following our lead – they are here to show us. We are simply there to guide them in leading the way into the new earth, embodying a higher level of consciousness.

My personal journey with my daughter has been just that. I knew she was here to show me, and that is exactly how I parent her while parenting myself again. I realised early on after having her that I had birthed another level of consciousness that was being reflected back at me, giving me the chance to now mother and nurture myself as well as her. I could not parent her from the same level of consciousness that I was parented.

All that I see and experience in front of me is what I have put there energetically to reflect back to me what I need to witness in order for me to expand and grow further in my own evolution. There is no escaping your own evolution. It's just a question of how much are you resisting it.

The planet is my playground and I get to choose the reality I want to experience. So what do I want to see? What do I want to feel?

And how do I want to grow and expand my very being, which will result in the impact I have as part of a collective consciousness of humanity?

Truly living is through connection and is paramount to living a limitless life and being a continuous expansion of who you are. When we can connect to our core self regularly, we receive all the answers and guidance we could possibly need. We learn to trust in ourselves rather than relying on outside influences, other people's opinions and their belief structures, which may or may not be in line with our true beliefs. This was a big realisation for me and I finally decided that it was time to fully trust myself instead of continuously living in doubt. 2020 was when I finally made the choice to live fully and to trust my own emotional guidance system and no longer doubt it.

Our children are amazing souls that have the ability to trigger us. Part of truly living is to allow yourself to see what your child is trying to show you via the internal triggers. The triggers are the signposts to heal and release a particular pattern that is no longer serving you or them and that way you take a leap forward in your own evolutionary process.

Connecting back to our source allows us to evolve in conjunction with the planet we live on.

Is attacking ourselves and each other the answer to our evolution? I suspect not. Is replaying experiences we had in our life experience the answer to our evolution as human beings on this planet? No!

To step into a new paradigm of living, truly living, it is time to offload all of those self-destructive and self-limiting patterns.

I think if you asked most human beings on the planet they would like to see peace in our external world but lack the true understanding and realisation that peace can only come from the inside of you. That is how we begin to see peace. In our external reality, we create it.

There is no end to the abundance you can experience, and equally there is no end to the feeling of shortage and need if you choose to focus on an energy of lacking. You have the power to manifest your experiences all the time. What are you choosing to manifest? Abundance or not having enough?

True aligned manifestation begins with surrender. You manifest from a different level of consciousness. We as human beings are a manifestation. Our souls manifested into a physical form to have these powerful experiences. NOW is the time.

I share all of this with you on a basic level because it has been my experience. Not only have I enjoyed reading for over 20 years about manifesting, but I have also always been able to manifest anything I wanted – which hasn't always been a good thing I might add! It's only over the last few years that I have begun to intentionally manifest.

I now live my life from a totally different level of consciousness as a sovereign being, despite what might play out in the external world. I get to choose my reality. I get to choose my reality every day; I get to be a blank canvas if I choose and start again. I do not need to beat myself up for getting things wrong, because there is nothing to get wrong when you expand your awareness beyond polarity. This is how I try to be a mother to my daughter and raise her to know she is a sovereign being, a freethinker.

We came into this world free, innocent and expressive, knowing only love. But we have forgotten this. It's now time to remember who and what you are. You have the freedom and choice to be that way – but only if you allow yourself to.

We are in a time that is our greatest opportunity to shift our collective consciousness to really embody the level of consciousness that our children are. They are the ones that are the guides for us to evolve.

Go ahead, start looking where you can live more consciously and begin co-creating with the universe. The universe is there to support you when you ask, align, allow and receive.

Go ahead and begin the journey to truly living from a more evolved space within you.

Journal

Ask yourself now what it would be like to finally truly live in accordance with the earth and co-create and step into your dreams.

We live in an abundant universe, it's as simple as that.

When I mention the word 'abundance', ask yourself, 'What does abundance mean to me?'

The planet is your playground and you get to choose the reality you want to experience. So what do you want to see? What do you want to feel?

How do you want to grow and expand your very being, which will impact the collective consciousness of humanity?

How are you creating your own reality? What emotion or thought process is driving your reality?

Chapter 10

Oneness

The symbiotic connection to all

Oneness is pure presence and connectivity to all.

Oneness is seeing everything as the whole you.

A s I explained before, you can allow yourself to access presence through the process of surrender. You access the experience of Oneness through opening the energy gateways known as chakras. Before I go any further, I would like to expand on chakras and dimensions and talk to you about the 3rd, 4th and 5th dimension as it is part of our current evolutionary process for ascension. We are all as a collective currently opening up energetically to higher realms which is known as the ascension process. I briefly talked about the 3rd dimensional chakras in chapter 3. It is time now to activate your 5th dimensional chakras.

In brief, the 3rd dimension is the material world governed mostly by fear. In this dimension, we accumulate material things and then live in fear of losing them all. We experience fear of losing control, not being secure and not feeling good enough. We lack trust in people. We define ourselves by what we possess and what we do for a living. We believe in separation from our creator, source energy. While we are not one with source energy, we cannot experience Oneness with all that is.

We hold beliefs of scarcity and having to fight or work hard to get what we need because there is not enough for everyone. Beliefs held about life being a competition. Beliefs in certain roles for men and women. I am quite sure you will relate to most of that description.

The 4th dimension is known as the dream world and the Astral Plane. This dimension is less dense and more fluid than the third dimension. It hosts the illusion of duality, and the ego is able to exist also here. It is the dimension of time. The fourth dimension connects darkness and light.

The 5th dimension is based on love. It is the plane of Oneness where we feel connection to everyone and everything around us. In the 5th dimension, we live in unity consciousness. We recognise ourselves as individuals and as part of a whole.

The 5th dimensional chakra column is designed to provide access to the higher frequencies moving you forward on your evolutionary development into a soul-embodied human being.

THE FIFTH DIMENSIONAL CHAKRAS

STELLAR GATEWAY
COLOUR: gold
POSITION: eighteen inches above the top of the head
Is the chalice of receptivity for all incoming stellar vibrations and information.

THE SOUL STAR
COLOUR: magenta
POSITION: six inches above the top of the head
Contains the blueprint for all of our spiritual gifts.

CAUSAL
COLOUR: moon white
POSITION: rear of the head
Is our full connection to the angelic realm.

THE CROWN
COLOUR: liquid gold
POSITION: top of the head
Receives information processed by the higher self and is fed by the upper three transcendent chakras.

THIRD EYE
COLOUR: emerald crystal
POSITION: forehead
Is our manifestation point. The receptivity centre that puts information we receive into tangible reality.

THROAT
COLOUR: bright blue
POSITION: throat
Very powerful, taking the vibration of thought patterns into spoken manifestation.

HEART
COLOUR: bright white
POSITION: chest
The most powerful energy centre. Here is where pure love is accessed and created.

SOLAR PLEXUS
COLOUR: bright gold
POSITION: solar plexus
The fifth dimensional solar plexus is known as the feeler within the body. It accesses all forms of surrounding vibrations and analyses them.

NAVEL
COLOUR: bright orange
POSITION: just below the belly button
Using this chakra consciously, you will fully know the complete

interconnection between oneself and all other forms of life on this planet.

SACRAL
COLOUR: pink
POSITION: sacrum
Can be quite challenging to clear. Contains most of the modern-day challenges, those still working through financial and relationship issues will be clearing through initiations held here.

BASE
COLOUR: platinum
POSITION: base of the spine
The Master I AM presence here on Earth.

EARTH STAR
COLOUR: deep grey or silver
POSITION: below the feet
This is where deep grounding takes place.

FIFTH DIMENSIONAL COLUMN WITH ARCHANGEL MICHAEL'S SWORD

Just for a moment allow yourself to expand your energy out beyond your physical body and even if you don't believe, just allow yourself to imagine that your body has energy centres which are like vortexes. I like to focus on the 12-chakra system as we can access our connection to the entire universe once we open them up to the oneness of everything, to total connection.

I truly believe now is the time to explore this part of yourself. To begin to experience yourself as an energy being first. I can assure you that you are energy and you are able to experience the chakras.

This has been my experience, and that experience is my evidence. I choose not to focus on the old science that doesn't support this truth. However, it's worth knowing that the new science does. In my life, I have had so many experiences to give me enough evidence. I have not just read about it. Experience is true knowledge and no one should diminish your experiences just because they may not understand it. We are lucky as we are living in a time where the new science is merging with spirituality. Go ahead and check it out for yourself. Quantum physics is talking so extensively about the energetics of everything.

As you now step into the idea of Oneness, allow your whole – your mind, body and spirit – your true self to integrate that very idea of what Oneness would feel like as an experience. What would it be like to live in that vast space of Oneness? Who would you be? Perhaps in that moment you can feel the experience of freedom and a knowing that we are in one vast energetic space with unlimited potential. And we can create. We are all born creators.

If you are coming from a 3rd dimensional level of consciousness, it can be very difficult to fathom the very idea of Oneness, especially if you are trying to understand Oneness intellectually. Perhaps you struggle to get your head around it? So it makes it seem nonsense, which it would, coming from an intellectual thinking space, I totally hear you. I tried for years putting my experiences into some intellectual, analytical processes and it simply blocked and denied the most beautiful experiences I was capable of having. As I mentioned to you earlier in the book, the ego or analytical mind becomes the block for universal intelligence to be accessed.

Oneness means everything and more as, let's face it, there are many more worlds we can create. Oneness means the ultimate connection to all that is, all there ever was, and all there is ever going to be. There isn't anything that does not hold the same consciousness as you. You are connected to all.

When we allow ourselves to step out of the linear thinking of past and future and be present in the now moment, transformation can take place.

Being present allows to us to continue to integrate within us anything that we may be processing energetically whether that be emotional, mental or spiritual. We can also process experiences and feelings that have often been associated with soul events that have occurred before this particular lifetime. Energy never dies, and time does not exist in the way we think it does. So many of those lifetimes are still occurring simultaneously.

We have always been under the illusion that the universe is outside us, when actually we access it within us, within every cell, and it is forever expanding and transforming. Just to bring in some child-like fun think of Buzz Lightyear in *Toy Story*! As he says, 'To infinity and beyond!' Those words sum it up, really. The more we go within, the more we are able to access everything: wisdom, knowledge, guidance and infinite intelligence.

CONNECTION

Just to reiterate again, my truth and understanding around the word 'spirituality' is connection. Connection to what, or whom, you may ask. YOU!!!!!! You are the whole; you are the experience, the everything within, you are the universal system encased in a physical vessel; you hold everything that ever was, ever is and is ever going to be, deeply within your heart as the source of ultimate divine intelligence.

As you connect fully into your heart's intelligence, you can begin to trust your inner knowing. Have you ever had an experience where you knew something so wholeheartedly but didn't listen to it, to later see it come true? That is always a good way to receive validation that you are an intuitive being and you can trust your guidance.

Connection is fundamental to living a balanced and authentic life. I feel very strongly about connection, as it has so many facets to it. Mainly it embodies one fundamental truth – that life without connection is lost and disempowered.

You, as a human being, are made up of exactly the same energy as the whole universe, pure creation.

Imagine what it would be like to see your life flow with ease, having patience, tolerance and understanding for yourself and others. Try seeing everyone as an extension of or mirror to yourself and as your greatest teacher.

We are one consciousness manifested into physical reality.

Connection to the divine is found within us and is otherwise known as awareness or consciousness.

Connection is what humans all strive for, especially in times of experiencing feelings of separation. We are seeing separation at its peak now, being promoted through fear-based beliefs and structures. Equally, this is driving an inner desire for many of us to truly connect now.

Connection allows us to move back to being more of a collective consciousness and community and supporting each other as one.

Perhaps you were not even aware that you are possibly having an awakening experience during these times we are in and/or until you started to read some of this book. That you are here reading this means that the spark within you is ready to awaken now.

You may have learned in school that energy is vibration and frequency, if you paid attention, unlike me! I wasn't ready to learn it intellectually then. I talk about vibrations and frequencies a lot because I work with energy first now and I live my life like that. My channelled writing informed me that Oneness has no vibratory resonance with words, as words can be so limiting. Perhaps this is why art is a much better way to portray the energetic vibrations, as it is experienced through feeling and an undisputed knowing. Art has energy imprinted into it that will connect with the energy of the person experiencing the art.

Back in 2017 as I was channelling information through my meditations and journalling, I noticed a tremendous shift taking place within me. I was getting ready to really channel from the energy vibration of love instead of any particular guide I may have had. Here is what it channelled to me back in 2017:

*We wish you well on your path. We are
now about to hand you over to beings
of a much higher realm where you will
be so safe and your family too. It is
without doubt you are going to do great
things now and true leadership work.*

*Traverse safely on your trip dear one.
We have enjoyed our journey with you
but we must go now as you have higher
work which is above our vibration. The
new vibration is crazy and enlightening
beyond words and regular belief. It is
here that you will get your true abilities
to use when working with others, this
transition is necessary for you, please
do not be alarmed, it its totally safe
for you. The new ones will introduce
themselves to you very soon, stay open
for them to emerge. Thank you dear one.*

Shortly after that information had come through, I received my
new guidance:

*We are from the realm of Oneness which
you are to work from now and forever.
We are beings of pure enlightenment
which you are now embodying (no
ego necessary at this point). Please be
graceful with this energy and use wisely.
It is not important what others think,
all you have to do is stay humble and use
what we give you. Help is always at hand
dear one. Our name is transitory and
is not important, there is no vibratory
resonance for a name, it is simply an
energy, pure essence has no name.
Go forth and work, follow our lead.*

Now it's time to really discover the true nature of identity and how it's forever metamorphosing. One true identity which is love.

Having channelled that information, I was left feeling totally blessed. In the core of my very being has always been the desire to be of service, and I felt that my journey up to this point had all been worth it. I now just needed to step fully into trust.

Also during 2017, I had a couple of spontaneously profound moments of Oneness. The first one happened one evening, when I was having fun with my daughter. In this moment I had an experience of truly witnessing and seeing her as a conscious being while simultaneously seeing myself exactly the same. It was totally beyond the physical. I was experiencing the essence of who we are from a connected space. In that moment, all separation or the illusion of separation had vanished and there was only the experience of one. I realised and in fact remembered in that moment that I was her and she was me, merged totally as one with nothing separating us energetically. In that moment also I had a realisation that I could actually re-parent myself as I was parenting her and allow myself to start from the beginning as I undid my early conditioned foundation.

In just a flash of a moment, there were so many profound realisations. Watch out for them because they happen.

Another experience of Oneness happened not long after that one, as I was walking down the street. Again, it was like I had merged or morphed with everything around me. The feeling was so divine and blissful, words cannot do it justice.

When you experience Oneness, you will not have the capacity to doubt it in the moment.

You may of course fall back into unconsciousness, old behaviours and conditioned ways of living. This happens and is actually quite normal, especially as we are all having a human experience. This is where so many practices can be incorporated into your daily existence to allow you to hear and see your world at a more expansive level of consciousness. It's like when you exercise your physical body or like fine-tuning an instrument when you want to use it – we need to practise with our energetic body.

I am so thrilled to categorically say now that Oneness can actually be experienced without having the influence of chemicals to bring on the experience. However, I am not saying that it is wrong if people choose to use natural medicines to journey into Oneness. I know natural medicines used in shamanic practices to support healing can be so powerful in the most nurturing setting with people that know what they are doing. I must admit I have often thought about having an experience like that with a group of experienced shamans. I have come to understand that I am a modern-day shaman and I am being guided to use these gifts to serve. They are not my gifts to withhold for my journey, they are to be shared with the collective consciousness of humanity. And it is ok and safe for me to come out of the shamanic closet, so to speak.

As I touched on earlier about the souls of other lifetimes being experienced simultaneously, I have had repeated experiences of times that I was persecuted for the wisdom I shared.

I believe that deep down we are all really striving to know the full magnitude of who and what we actually are. You are an extraordinary being having this human experience. There is a deep, unconscious desire that is desperately trying to make itself known in the conscious mind. You are already a perfect creation of source energy that just wants to be witnessed and seen mostly by yourself. You are the one.

Perhaps it's time we redefined our mental understanding of the belief around 'perfect' and what that means to us. Is perfection achieved when we receive validation from another? Or is it when we choose to validate ourselves as that Oneness and presence?

AWARENESS

Allow your awareness to focus on noticing where your thinking may be on what you are lacking. Lack thinking can show up in so many areas of your life. This way of thinking can be so unconscious.

Be a witness to the kind of conversations you may have and how much the idea of the 'lack of' comes into it.

Have a day allowing your awareness to shift at any moment to notice where you are truly abundant. Abundance is experienced in the moment. Notice where you are always taken care of in that moment and have everything you possibly need. The more you focus on abundance, the more you invite into your life.

When we are in lack, we have separated ourselves from source energy. When we are in abundance, we are connected and trusting. Looking at lack and abundance allows us to see another level of what beliefs we hold.

Journal

Allow yourself to really flow with the journalling questions, don't hold back.

Grab your journal and begin a daily gratitude and appreciation practice. You will find that it's powerful.

What would it be like to live in the vast space of Oneness and unlimited potential?

Who would you be, and what would you do differently with your life experience?

Where are you being truly authentic? Look at your relationships and also the relationship you have with yourself.

Authenticity flows through when you have a genuine connection to the real you.

Have you ever had an experience where you knew something so wholeheartedly but didn't listen to it, to later see it come true? Journal an experience you may have had and write about what made you doubt it.

CHANNELLING

Grab your journal and have a go at free-writing. Become an open channel for your higher self to flow through.

Do a short meditation opening up the heart by breathing and focusing on the heart.

Perhaps ask one question to the heart and just allow the words to flow onto the paper without analysing it. There is no right or wrong here. Even if you write a few words, you have begun the process.

Everything I suggest is practice.

Worlds

Old world and new world

W e can create worlds! I am the creator of the world I want to see and experience, and so are you.

So how do you create the world you want to see on the outside of you? You go within and do the work in there. There are infinite possibilities that can be accessed within you, it's about clearing away anything inside that no longer serves you or the greater good of humanity. And you will probably find that it is where all the beliefs that do not support the world you want to see and experience are.

Everything is happening NOW. There is no past or future in the way you are conditioned to believe. So, if everything is happening now, then you can create now by using your imagination and emotional guidance system, your inner GPS.

Imagine for a moment that the children that are being born now are from the future. What a crazy notion that is, hey? When we can view that idea from a perspective of consciousness, the possibility of the children being from the future is true. Today's children embody such an expanded level of consciousness that it is proving more and more challenging to integrate them into outdated education systems. These systems seem to suppress more children rather than allowing them to thrive. The systems as we know them are beginning to crumble and collapse because of expanded levels of consciousness filtering through to our planet now. This means anything that was created from a lower level of consciousness cannot sustain itself any longer.

We now need to build systems that are expansive enough to cater for the magnitude of awareness these children have and to support them in expressing themselves freely. They are the future – which is why we must allow them to bring forth the awareness and the knowledge they hold in their hearts. This will ultimately bring forth our new world.

As a mother you are a guide and a guardian to help them become their fullest expression, as you begin to fully express your own true essence.

When we truly remember our own innate ability to co-create with the universe and know that the outside world is merely a holographic illusion or mirror of what we hold within us, then we can totally move mountains and create the world or worlds we wish to see. I choose a world where love, freedom, sovereignty and inclusion take centre stage. And the children we are birthing are the answer to showing us that.

Creating and living in a world where we embrace abundance and joy and live in connected union to all that is within the universe is achievable and happens NOW. It's not something you have to wait for. You can be that person that uses every ability you were born with and access it through the vibration of LOVE.

Think for a few moments about what brings you joy and appreciation. Focus on it and breathe it into your very being. You always have a choice at any moment to change your point of attention and attraction. This is the law of attraction.

For most of my life I tried to fit into other people's perception of the world and was expected to share their belief that there is only one world. This led me to constantly look for where I might fit in and what label I would need to put on myself in order to fit in and be accepted there.

Constantly looking outside of myself only made me into more of a chameleon. This is an ability many of us have, we morph into the energy of others, taking on many of the characteristics of another. Is this perhaps to give us the feeling of fitting in and feeling included? I'm not fully sure. Perhaps it is our innate ability to change with the energy of that person and translate their energy signature to better connect. I can now see how that ability works in my sessions with others. I use myself as the channel to translate the other person and aid their understanding of their 'self' as they go through their clearing and integration process and awakening. As I continued to look outside myself to find where I might fit in, it just brought more of the experience of not fitting in. I will never find that place because all I had to do was fit my entire being or higher self into my physical vessel and create my world that I would totally fit in to. As I said before, this physical experience is about fully realising and experiencing the highest version of yourself and witnessing the full magnitude of who and what you are. Your world, your experience.

I became aware quite early in my life that the media was very good at portraying and obsessively feeding one version of reality and that we should all fit into that version. This is simply not true. However, I did question and doubt my realisations for a very long time because I didn't have people around me to validate a lot of them, which led me to feel alienated. So I often slipped back into my unconscious self, probably more for self-preservation in a way, even though that kept me trapped in my self-destructive patterns of living in and experiencing a world of darkness. This just highlights that if you are experiencing a world of darkness, then the way to free yourself from that world is to simply do the inner clearing work as I have outlined throughout this book. Do the work of healing and integrating lifetimes of experiences in this now moment. There are many facilitators that can offer healing techniques to guide you into stepping fully into your higher self where you create the world you want to experience, despite what you may observe around you.

Media is a mechanism to show you versions of reality you could choose to experience. But is that you having control over consciously choosing your reality? Or is it implanted information into your psyche, influencing your inner belief system? Are you making your own informed choices from your own inner guidance system? Or are you acting on your own unconscious thoughts that are triggered by many forms of external media and other people's opinions based on their own agendas, conditioning and belief structures?

As I realised more and more that I was creating my reality, what stood out for me was the insanity of being told to conform to some ruling, regimental system, fit into this label or that label. This regimental system was more often than not quite self-limiting and suppressed my ability to create. Labels are often placed on us in order for systems to control us. This is the old world that we now see crumbling.

I chose early on not to conform to orders coming from people who had absolutely no idea what my best interests actually were. Those governing that one reality or one common narrative via the media are so lost in the linear and 3rd dimensional state of being. Perhaps they want to keep people locked into a false sense of security and making us follow, like flocks of sheep. I would jump from one reality to another until I opted out and began to fully follow my internal guidance system that gives me the ability to create worlds and not follow old, outdated belief patterns that are just on repeat. It was time to fully opt out and get off the merry-go-round of repeat patterns and create new worlds. The moment I chose this was the moment my life experience was one of liberation, freedom and joy.

What increasingly came to my awareness was my ability to oscillate between so many different worlds, without even realising it. This is an amazing ability that we all have, by the way. What needed my attention and effort was techniques to ground my energy fully into my body, so I could be more in the present moment to bring forth and enjoy the fruits of my creations. My creations are experienced in the physical manifestation of the new world.

This brings me to talking about walking through many worlds through our consciousness. Actually, when it comes to our children, they are doing it all the time. Notice how often they daydream, not paying attention. These days this can be interpreted by some 'professionals' as an opportunity to put the label of Attention Deficit Disorder, known as ADD or Attention Deficit Hyperactivity Disorder, commonly known as ADHD, on a lot of these children. I prefer to think of ADHD as attention dialed into a higher dimension because that is what it really is. Whether or not it is required, it is followed by another cash injection to the pharmaceutical companies – but let's not get started on that one just yet, hey! Some of us have brains that are wired in such a different way, but that does not make us wrong. It means we need to find less linear ways of being and learning in order to facilitate us and understand how our neural activity is functioning from a higher perspective, and not to reach immediately for prescribed drugs. If I am honest, and going on my experience, prescribing drugs only serves to suppress and potentially create the next generation of drug addicts.

The world I witnessed as I grew up appeared to be run on fear, and I was experiencing fear from a felt perception as a child. I, like many children, was and still am an empath. This is actually a normal state of being, as we are sentient beings. I now fully understand I was not fully present in my body and never developed a relationship with it because the vibration of energy I was picking up at the time was not comfortable for me to hold in my body. So I would spend most of my time out of my body. This frequently happens when experiences are traumatic.

I was never taught that my body was part of me, part of the whole essence of me. Again, this is not about imparting blame anywhere. No one would have thought at that time that they had to help me understand this as for most people in those times it was just a given that I am just this physical being. And yet that was not how I experienced it. My awareness was profoundly centred around the fact that I was not just this physical being. I reiterate this with importance because growing up I saw and experienced my body as a separate entity to me, a bit of a hindrance that was keeping me trapped. I saw it as a parasite, eating away at itself, destroying itself. This links to the feeling of just wanting to go home and be free of this trap. This was contributing to the realities I was creating for myself.

I can traverse many different worlds through my consciousness and envision what sort of world I would like to see and experience. Oh, and by the way, so are you – believe it or not. Yes, you have that ability and all it takes is to give yourself permission to take the journey of remembering who and what you are once you open up. You can break away from the shackles and restrictions that have been programmed into you, mostly through the influence of media, and then passed on from person to person, believing they know best because those in power have said so.

As I wrote this section of the book, my daughter had a friend staying over and they were both questioning so many things. To hear them question so many things lit me up as this is the essence of pure curiosity and excitement. They were looking to me for the answers, but actually I just explored the questions more with them from a space of curiosity within me. This was something I had forgotten early on that I could do. When we open up to curiosity, we again harness our ability to create and not just believe what we are being told.

As we question, we intentionally open up new gateways to allow us to create worlds that we want and choose to experience.

The motto in our house is QUESTION EVERYTHING. If we question everything, then we grow.

As you read this, the world is going through the most monumental dismantling and shake-up. Remember, you are a part of that world. You cannot see or witness anything outside of yourself if it is not present within you. This is the reason why the changes and dismantling can only occur within you, and we then manifest the outer world we want and choose to see. This is not a new concept. Manifestation is our god-given ability, it is happening all the time and as a collective consciousness we have the ability to step into an amazing world. As we expand our individual consciousness from one of separateness to one of unity, we impact the world for the greater good. It's time to STOP relying on others to do it for you. I had to be the one to fully trust in my internal guidance system, to see where it has always served me for the highest good and to run with it.

What is the world you are creating? Or are you still waiting for some force outside yourself to bring it to fruition for you? Make the choice NOW to take full responsibility for your life experience. Children are born into this world full of innocence and purity, and we as adults are programmed to believe that it is up to us to teach the young. Actually we are here as guides to them and they are here to continuously show us how to evolve.

We grow up indoctrinated by adults' experiences of life and believe that everything they say is how life is and should be. Each individual is going to have their own unique experience and have qualities to share with the world. It's time to drop the belief that we have to be so competitive. Have a go at noticing other people's qualities and begin to collaborate to make your external world a better place.

Stop the action of fighting for freedom – you are freedom. What this means is to stop the internal battle which is projected onto the outside reality. Collaborate with the natural order, the natural world. This is true liberation and freedom. True sovereignty. Nature will provide everything you need in any moment when you align with your higher guidance system. Be sovereign.

The natural world operates on the vibration of love. We are the natural world, and every ounce of our genetic make-up is connected to this evolutionary leap we are all currently experiencing.

Allow the love that your children embody to mirror back to you the love you had forgotten and always had access to in your own heart. As you begin to unlock your own heart from the self-imposed prison, you will experience a world you have long desired to see. Go forth and enter your heart-based reality, a world based on love.

Journal

Are you making your own informed choices from your own inner guidance system? Or are you making choices from unconscious thoughts programmed from many forms of external media and other people's opinions based on their own agendas, conditioning and belief structures? A good way to notice whether you are making your own intuitive decisions is whether you are questioning or in conflict with yourself.

Take a few moments to journal about what truly brings you joy and appreciation.

As we question, we intentionally open up new gateways to allow us to create worlds we want and choose to experience. Allow your awareness to shine on what you may be questioning now, and perhaps there may be questions that are on repeat. Also allow yourself to notice how your body feels when you ask a question. The body is very good at giving you an answer.

CHAPTER 12

Legacy

I decided to include a chapter about my legacy purely to give you a space to ask yourself, 'What will your legacy be?'

I wanted to share mine with you, as by doing so, I can acknowledge the courage it took for me to look at it and write it out. Not only that but also the courage it has taken to share it with others, no matter what they thought. What they thought is really none of my business.

Perhaps as you read this part, you might make some notes as you look at what your legacy might be. Go on – be bold, think about it, and have a look at what yours could be.

As I began to write this chapter, it made me wince with that uncomfortable sense of 'Who am I to even think (ego-based) that I could leave a legacy?' I also smiled because I felt within the depths of my heart that there is and always has been a greater purpose for the experience of my existence. It would have been a complete waste of all of the previous life experiences I have had not to believe that I could formulate some sort of legacy. I know that the trials, tribulations and moments of enlightenment in my life experience have all been worth it.

I would like my legacy to be that I played a big role in standing up for the truth about our human and spiritual evolution and understanding levels of consciousness and realities. I want to help smoothe the way for the integration process of the consciousness being presented in many children that are being given the labels of Autism, ADD and ADHD.

I want to take part in more research around Autism in relation to levels of consciousness and provide a support network for mothers who are birthing children that embody profound levels of consciousness. I want to provide the support via one-to-one settings and group work for the mothers who journey through their evolutionary process moving back to the energy and consciousness of Love. I also want my legacy to be that I helped shine a light on the fact that mental illness and symptoms of Autism did not and do not need to be treated so heavily with pharmaceuticals. My legacy will have been that I played my part within the collective that can provide new knowledge and new understandings.

I would like people to remember me for my humility, drive and determination to seek and experience truth and know that, no matter what my mistakes were, the fundamental reason for my life was to experience truth and joy. And that I shared with others by being an authentic example, despite the challenges and difficulties I had encountered. That I still continued to stand strong in my convictions of the truth and show how I navigated through the challenges. I would like people to remember me for my passion and love for the children on this planet and my belief in both their and our collective ability to raise the vibration here by allowing us to embody higher levels of consciousness and experience a new earth filled with love and joy.

I would love to see humanity living a more connected existence and harness their god-given gifts of life to manifest all the possibilities within them for the greater good. And to see the children be free to really bring about an expanded version of consciousness. I would love to see people understanding what true oneness and connectedness means, by ways of living that existence.

I would like to see the reduction if not the complete eradication of depressions, suicides and the mental illness rates that we are currently seeing. I would like to be a part of bringing forth new understandings to be shared, helping people to feel empowered and to know how to practise what is being shared with the belief it will make a difference to their life. I would love to see who we really are, as powerful transformative beings with all humanity living more joyfully and in alignment. I would love to see the overuse of medication in children reduced, only used if totally necessary, or abolished all together.

I also want to leave all the books I have written and the sessions I have taken part in for others to use so that they can serve to help them look back and to see how far we have progressed in our process of evolution.

My spiritual path has certainly been arduous, but clearly a very necessary one to get me to a place of really connecting with my core and that of the collective consciousness of the children as I lived from my child-like self of wonder again.

The gift I would like to leave for others after this journey is the example of anything is possible and it is possible to live in pure joy and love. I would also like to leave all the love that I put into caring about the path ahead for our amazing children of this world and how I helped them to be heard and supported through their missions in life. I want to leave behind good memories for my child, for her to have the knowledge and realisation of how much she impacted my life experience for the greater good, how blessed I am for her to have chosen me to be her guide and for her to know that she gave me the opportunity to experience real love within myself.

Conclusion

As we fully integrate every aspect of ourselves, we elevate our collective consciousness. Remember, we are LOVE and ONE consciousness made manifest.

Are you ready to enter a new paradigm and a completely new way of being to help bring forth the beautiful world our children have come here to live in unity with? All you need is the willingness to remember who and what you are.

I am ready.

So allow me to be the first one to welcome you to the new paradigm of pure creation.

What world will you create NOW?

It's time for you to go and create the systems that serve for the highest good of all humankind.

Acknowledgements

I would like to begin by thanking everyone I have encountered throughout my life experience so far, you have all been profound teachers.

I thank all of the mentors and guides I have had to get me to the point of finally writing this book. There have been many mentors throughout my life and for that I am deeply grateful. Words really do not convey the love and gratitude I feel.

I would like to say a huge thank-you to my husband Mike for supporting me, and always believing in me. A big thank-you goes to my writing coach Isabelle Izard. She never gave up on encouraging me to keep going, especially when I wanted to throw in the towel. She showed me so much love and nurture throughout the whole journey of writing this book. She provided a space where I could just be and unravel all of the thoughts and emotions that blocked me from writing. I would like to thank my very good friend Anna for providing a special space for us to proofread the book together. Those connected moments were truly special and I will hold them in my heart forever. We certainly did journey through the book together. My heartfelt thanks to my editor Joy Coutts, without whom this book would not flow as freely as it does. Joy's comments, loving critique and guidance was invaluable. Joy knew how important it was to me to keep my own voice held within the words I have written.

A final thank-you goes to my incredible daughter, who has blessed me with her presence and inspires me everyday. When I envision the future I see all that she embodies, love and joy.

I trust that this book will provide the love that I have received while writing it. My only wish is that it will serve for the highest good of all who read it. Know now that you are on the path of your own awakening process to fully embody all of who and what you are for the purpose of the evolution of humanity.

About the Author

Helen Fisher was born in Sheffield in the UK.

From being a young child, Helen felt in the depths of her core a profound purpose in life and has a passion for exploring consciousness and existence. She always felt that she was not just a physical body but was here to be part of something big happening on our planet. She couldn't quite put her finger on it in her early years. As time passed by, she realised what was going to happen: the great awakening and shift in consciousness.

Helen spent 23 years working in health care but this did not fulfil that deep desire in her heart to be of greater service. She experienced her first spiritual awakening in her early 20s following a complete nervous breakdown because of battling with addiction. From there she began her spiritual and healing journey. She realised she was part of being a pattern changer within the generational and ancestral lineage.

She continued to work in her profession while studying spirituality, healing, coaching and mentoring. Helen finally left that profession in 2017. She now follows her genuine passion and vocation, which is to support energetically sensitive mothers and children that present with the labels of Autism, ADHD and ADD. Helen also supports mothers through their own awakening process.

Helen's practice mirrors all the tools and techniques that she has used on her own spiritual and healing journey. She too is an energetically sensitive mother with an energetically sensitive child. Helen has always known that the children are the answer to seeing our new world manifest through embodying higher levels of consciousness.

Today Helen works as a Spiritual Teacher, Energy Healer and HeartMath Coach, and is now a writer and author.

Helen lives a simple life in North Cornwall with her husband and daughter. She home educates her daughter and continues to follow her dreams. Her passion is being the example for her daughter to align with her true soul path and follow her own dreams.

HOW TO CONTACT AND WORK WITH HELEN

Helen offers 1:1 sessions as a package. Sessions are held on line or at her home.

Sessions include:

- Remote healing for either mother or child or both, followed by 1:1 feedback
- In person healing for mother and/or child
- 90-minute 1:1 energy integration
- 60-minute HeartMath coaching

You can book a free 30-minute discovery call with Helen via the below contact details.

E-mail: helen@helenlfisher.com

Website: helenlfisher.com

Instagram: @quantum.heartmath.coach

Sign up to my newsletter at: eepurl.com/g3GUWr

Milton Keynes UK
Ingram Content Group UK Ltd.
UKHW020800110224
437528UK00010BA/89